# MARCHING BANDS AND DRUMLINES

◄ *Secrets of Success from the Best of the Best* ►

## PAUL BUYER

Published by
Meredith Music Publications
a division of G.W. Music, Inc.
4899 Lerch Creek Ct., Galesville, MD 20765
http://www.meredithmusic.com

Chapter opener photo: © 2007 Chris Scredon/iStockphoto.com
Text and cover design: Shawn Girsberger

International Standard Book Number: 978-1-57463-151-7
Library of Congress Control Number: 2009920455
Printed and bound in U.S.A.

# Contents

# CHAPTER 8  Evaluating Recruiting and Retention . 93

# CHAPTER 9  Crunching the Numbers . . . . . . . . . . . 109

# Bibliography. . . . . . . . . . . . . . . . . . . . . . . . . . . . . . . . 115

# About the Author . . . . . . . . . . . . . . . . . . . . . . . . . . . 117

# Acknowledgments

I have always been told that to be successful, surround yourself with successful people. As Eden Froust pointed out so eloquently, "Relationships create the fabric of our lives. They are the fibers that weave all things together." I am very fortunate to have an inner circle of friends and family who made it possible for me to do the research for this book. I would like to thank them for their support, encouragement, and belief in the project.

First, thank you to my amazingly supportive and understanding wife, April. Her passion for her students and for excellent teaching inspires me every day. Thank you to my parents: Richard, Andrea, Kris, and Ken, my brother Jason, my sister Kennedy, and my Grandmothers Rose Radlove and Emily Mann for their constant love, support, and encouragement.

Thank you to my Clemson family: Rick Goodstein, Mark Spede, Brian Sproul, and Mark Hosler, for providing me the rich laboratory of experiences that helped shaped this project, and to James Barker, Dori Helms, and Chip Egan, for their administrative support. To Mike Sammons, who began as my sabbatical replacement and became a dear friend, colleague, and sounding board for many of the ideas in this book. I am forever grateful to Mike for leading my students while I was away and for giving them a great experience. I would also like to thank my travel team: Larry Sloan, Sonja Massey, and Susan Kaplar for their guidance as travel agents and business managers.

I would like to extend a special thanks to my major teachers and mentors, Gary Cook, Erwin Mueller, and Michael Balter for always believing in me and for teaching me about percussion, leadership, and life. Their impact on this book is significant.

Thank you to Staci Stokes at Pro-Mark, Bruce Jacoby at Remo, Nick Petrella at Sabian, and David Suter at Yamaha for their leadership in the industry and educational support.

Of course none of this would have been possible without the incredible hosts I had at each school. These individuals welcomed me to their campus, made me feel at home, and took time out of their incredibly busy schedules to help me with my research. When it was time for the directors to introduce me to their students, I went from "Who is that guy?" to feeling like a member of their family. I'd like to extend my sincere gratitude and appreciation to all the wonderful leaders I met and the new friends I made: Frank Wickes, Linda Moorhouse, Roy King, and Ben Chamberlain at Louisiana State; Neal Flum and Ken Ozzello at Alabama; Bob Buckner and Matt Henley at Western Carolina; John Madden and Jon Weber at Michigan State; Jon Woods, Jon Waters and Gary Hodges at Ohio State; Nick Williams, Paul Rennick, Frank Nedley, and Matt Filosa at North Texas; and Jay Rees, Saul Aguilar, Vicente Lopez, and Debbie Lewis at Arizona.

Lastly, I would like to thank the Clemson University Tiger Band and my percussion students, past and present, for their incredible commitment and passion for this project. They are truly the ones who inspired me to grow and learn more about how we do what we do on and off the field.

—*Paul Buyer, July 2008*

# Introduction

I have been a sports fan all my life. Growing up in the Chicago area, I followed the Cubs, Bears, and Bulls on a regular basis. In high school I played on the golf team and was a percussionist in the band. In college, I started teaching drumlines and later marched and taught drum and bugle corps—Star of Indiana and Dutch Boy, respectively. As I became more involved with marching percussion at the college level, I started to notice that the collaboration between marching band and football was becoming a unique laboratory of study. The more I explored, the more interested I became in the lessons common to sports, music, and life.

I have studied leadership for several years, and it has quickly become a passion. Many of the lessons I teach my drumline during the season are about life. These are not lessons on stick heights, timing, or technique, but lessons on teamwork, commitment, and accountability. These are lessons that, hopefully, my students will apply to their lives as they prepare for their careers. Marching percussion and marching band activities can serve as a vehicle for teaching our students some of life's most valuable lessons.

Many of you may remember the 2007 college football season as one of the craziest in recent years. From Appalachian State's opening game upset over Michigan to LSU becoming the first two-loss team to win a BCS National Championship, the landscape of college football was never more unpredictable.

During what ESPN dubbed, the "Season of Upsets," I was on sabbatical visiting seven college marching bands around the country doing research on how their drumlines achieve performance excellence. Spending roughly a week at each school, I attended rehearsals, meetings, and football games and interviewed the band directors, drumline instructors, and section leaders. For three months I observed how other percussion instructors and band directors rehearse, teach, lead, and communicate with their bands and drumlines.

I was most interested in learning how other bands rehearsed and prepared for game day. My purpose was to learn about each drumline's goals, expectations, leadership style, work ethic, practice habits, rehearsal techniques, rehearsal schedule, performance preparation, repertoire, facilities, instrumentation, and traditions. To put it simply, I wanted to find out how everybody else "does it." I wanted to evaluate myself as an educator and a leader, and see how my program stacked up against the best. I wanted to learn from some of the top college marching bands in the country so my students and I could grow and improve, and now I would like to share what I learned with you.

Since 1998, I have served as Director of Percussion at Clemson University in Clemson, South Carolina. One of my primary responsibilities has been to direct and arrange for the Clemson Drumline. While fewer college percussion professors are teaching the drumline in addition to running the percussion studio, I continue to find great challenge and fulfillment in the leadership and teambuilding aspects of the activity. This is what I enjoy most—taking a group of individuals each year and molding them into a team. In my article, *Lessons Learned On and Off the Field*, I discuss nine lessons students and instructors must adopt in order for a marching percussion ensemble to reach its full potential and achieve a high level of excellence. "A drumline that works hard, prepares well, plays with confidence, is consistent and committed, demonstrates a positive attitude, has strong leadership, works together as a team, and knows how to stay focused can expect to achieve the goals it sets for itself."

For years, I have been fascinated with how certain sports teams achieve and sustain a culture of excellence. Some programs I have followed closely include Duke and Arizona basketball, Ohio State and Southern California football, and professional franchises like the New England Patriots and San Antonio Spurs. I always figured if I was a coach, I would make every effort to study these teams in depth and try to apply their philosophies and standards to my own program.

## The Model

The idea for this project was inspired by a book written in 2004 by sports reporter and author, Brian Curtis entitled, *Every Week a Season,* where Curtis "takes readers on an unprecedented whirlwind tour of NCAA Division 1 football."

Curtis visited nine big-time college football programs in nine weeks with the intention of getting to the "beating heart of college football" by going behind the scenes and taking readers inside team meetings, on the sidelines during practices and games, and in the locker room. Curtis also got to know the coaches—the leaders of their respective programs—and profiled their leadership style, communication skills, and relationship with their teams. These are the attributes I hope to bring to life in the world of college marching band drumlines.

In the forward to Curtis' book, former Michigan Football Coach Lloyd Carr states that he "was fascinated by how other coaches run their programs." This is, at its core, the thesis of this book. Because college marching bands generally do not compete, are not televised, do not have scouts attend games, and travel primarily within their own conference, it is at best challenging for instructors and students to be aware of what other bands are doing, how they are doing it, and where the top programs might reside.

## Selecting the Bands

So where *do* the top programs reside? With over twenty bands on my initial list, I decided to choose seven schools based on their home football schedules, diversity in location, athletic conference, and marching band tradition, and reputation for having an excellent marching band. What evolved was a list of schools that I believe are seven of the top college marching bands and drumlines in the country. They are:

Louisiana State University
University of Alabama
Western Carolina University
Michigan State University
Ohio State University
University of North Texas
University of Arizona

This list also represents the order in which I visited the schools, as the home football schedules and geographic proximity to Clemson worked very well. After deciding on the schools I wanted to visit, I wrote a formal letter to the band director and drumline instructor soliciting interest. I am proud to say that all the schools agreed to host me and no one declined my request. I then composed a detailed itinerary for each school including rehearsal schedules, interviews, and clinics, and then communicated at length with each band director throughout the planning process. I was intent on not being a bother, as I was fully aware of how busy the directors were going to be during the season. The only thing I asked for, in addition to their time, was a parking pass.

## It's Not Easy Being Green

Knowing my time on campus would be limited, I wanted to find a way to connect with the students and directors right away. I decided to visit the bookstore and buy a hat of each school which I would wear to rehearsals. This was a big hit among the students, as I was immediately welcomed into their band family. I also planned ahead and packed a shirt in each school's colors that I would wear to the football games. In September, October, and November, I became a fan of the Crimson Tide, the Catamounts, the Spartans, the Buckeyes, the Mean Green, and the Wildcats. Needless to say, it was easy for me to root for the Tigers in Death Valley during my stay in Baton Rouge!

During my visit to Michigan State, the Spartans played Indiana as I proudly wore green to root them on to victory. The next week I traveled to Ohio State, and as fate would have it, the Buckeyes were playing Michigan State, and MSU's band was making the trip to Columbus. I looked forward to wearing red to support the #1 team (at that time) in the nation, as well as seeing my new friends again from East Lansing. On the OSU practice field game day morning, I reunited with the Michigan State staff. Jon Weber, MSU's drumline instructor, waved, came over to me, and shouted, "Paul, you look better in green!" I smiled, shook his hand, and quickly replied, "Thanks Jon, but my real color is orange!"

## A Fly on the Wall

In the following pages, I hope to provide you with an inside look at seven of the top college marching bands and drumlines in the country. You will discover how Frank Wickes at LSU developed a tradition of excellence and how Jay Rees at Arizona built a culture of uncommon discipline. You will be given access to how Western Carolina's Bob Buckner and his staff incorporate a rock band into their show and how Alabama's Neal Flum collaborates with his four assistants. You will go behind the scenes at Ohio State as Jon Woods promotes extraordinary self-motivation and how Michigan State's Jon

Weber built a drumline so strong he had to turn away forty players. You will also experience the aura of North Texas, hear Paul Rennick's teaching philosophy, and finally understand the school's unique history of having two drumlines.

## Five Factors Influencing Excellence

After traveling to seven beautiful campuses, conducting over twenty inspiring interviews, and becoming part of each band's culture for a week, I discovered my research could be summarized into "Five Factors Influencing Excellence." The five factors are:

1. Culture
2. Staff and Student Leadership
3. Rehearsal Time
4. Number of Shows
5. Competitive Auditions

These factors are the main reasons why, I believe, college bands and drumlines achieve excellence or fall short of it. Granted, some factors like culture and leadership are under one's control, while others like rehearsal time and number of shows may not be. Let me to explain why these five factors are so important.

### *Culture*

According to ethnomusicologist Dorothea Hast, culture is defined as "a group's shared ways of experiencing, participating in, and making sense out of their world. Culture accounts for why these people over here think and act differently from those people over there."

From the moment I stepped onto the practice field, I could see, hear, and feel the unique culture of each marching band I visited. This feeling could be described as a dynamic or a "vibe" that resonated in the band's attitude, character, and work ethic. These attributes, working together, produced a powerful sense of pride in the bands. Pride in the uniform. Pride in the university. Pride in being a member of the organization. Pride in being good.

The students I observed were ambassadors of their culture as they exhibited a high level of buy-in to their leaders as well as to the philosophy and values of the organization. Buy-in is arguably one of the most important yet elusive qualities of building a culture of excellence. As Jim Collins, author of *Good to Great*, said of buy-in, "Do whatever you can to get the right people on the bus, the wrong people off the bus, and the right people in the right seats." From my observations, these programs generated buy-in primarily through trust and respect.

A band's culture is shaped by its standards. Standards define what is and is not acceptable in your program. The bands I observed had high standards including performing at a high level, showing up on time, practicing and being prepared, and treating others with respect. Standards set the bar for your program and act as a guide for making decisions. They influence behavior and instill discipline. According to Duke University head basketball coach Mike Krzyzewski,

> *Developing a culture means having a tradition that maintains the standards you want to define your program. A*

*successful development of culture means that you hear dif-*
*ferent voices echoing the same message throughout the or-*
*ganization—now, throughout the history of your program,*
*and into its future. But you cannot merely expect culture*
*to be a natural occurrence; it has to be taught and made*
*part of your everyday routine. Teaching culture is not just*
*the leader's task; everyone on the team is responsible for*
*passing on the values, standards, and tradition on to the*
*next generation.*

## Staff and Student Leadership

Former Secretary of State Colin Powell once said, "The performance of an organization is the ultimate measure of its
leader." How true that is. Without question, each band has
a culture that is a direct reflection of its leadership. All the
bands have exceptional band directors and drumline instructors—men and women who understand they are not just
teaching band, they are teaching people. They are giving
their students a life experience that goes beyond band and
even beyond music. They are simply using band as a vehicle.
Some of the life lessons that were emphasized by these extraordinary leaders include citizenship, teamwork, preparation, focus, commitment, and perseverance. To learn more
about the values and life lessons taught by all the bands, see
Chapter 3, *Teaching Life Lessons.*

I was especially impressed with the section leaders—students who have earned the respect of their directors and peers
and who have not only accepted the responsibility of leadership, but embraced it. During their interviews, the section
leaders were well-spoken, intelligent, and mature. Virtually

all of them said the hardest part about being a section leader was leading their peers and balancing their friendships with doing their job. They learned many things from their experience, including making difficult decisions, resolving conflicts, and confronting their teammates when necessary.

Most importantly, the student leaders buy into and share their director's vision and are truly extensions of the staff in words and actions. There is no doubt that to have an excellent college marching band, you need an excellent band director, as well as an excellent staff and student leaders who are on the same page and who buy into the philosophy of the program. Several schools like Michigan State, Ohio State, Western Carolina, and Arizona offer leadership courses or workshops for their student staff. It is here where student leaders learn the necessary leadership and teambuilding skills necessary to have a successful season each year and to pass on the culture of excellence to students coming into the program for the first time.

## Rehearsal Time

Few factors have more influence on a marching band's performance level than rehearsal time. Not surprisingly, the rehearsal schedules of the seven bands I visited vary significantly, with some rehearsing every day (Monday-Friday) to others just three times a week (MWF). The length of rehearsals range from ninety minutes to two hours and drumline rehearsal schedules varied as well, especially with the amount of sectional time. For a more detailed look at each band's rehearsal schedule, see Chapter 9, *Crunching the Numbers*.

Because rehearsal schedules differ so markedly from band to band, comparing performance levels is sometimes like comparing apples and oranges. But regardless of how *often* a band rehearses, the goal is always to perform at a high level of excellence. As much as rehearsal time impacts a band's performance level, it is, for the most part, out of the director's control. I have always found it ironic that life as a college marching band member can be so rushed, busy and frantic during a season that lasts nearly five months. Ask any college band director and he/she will tell you that there never seems to be enough rehearsal time. So how do the John Maddens and Ken Ozzellos of the world handle the challenge of rehearsal time? How do they get their students to learn so much material in such a short time? And how do some bands produce such a quality product on game day after only one week of preparation? One way they overcome these challenges and accomplish these goals is by focusing on the things they *can* control. According to Jeff Janssen, sports leadership expert at the University of North Carolina,

> *The question is not which obstacles can I point to as a legitimate excuse for why we aren't as successful as we could be, it's which opportunities do I need to focus on and expand to get us to where we'd like to be. The key is to put your energies toward the things you can control and impact rather than getting frustrated and discouraged by the ones you can't.*

## Number of Shows

The fourth factor influencing excellence which also varies from band to band is the number of shows performed. In 2007, the

Ohio State Marching Band performed seven different halftime shows, preparing a new show for every home game. Michigan State performed six, LSU five, and Alabama and North Texas three. At many of these schools, the number of shows the band performs is steeped in tradition and is expected by fans and alumni as well as the band members themselves.

Performing a large number of shows during a season can present many challenges for a college marching band. Without question, the biggest challenge is a lack of sufficient rehearsal time to learn, memorize, and clean the music and drill so the band can perform with confidence on game day. Another challenge is balancing the difficulty level of the music and drill with performance quality. In my article, *Balancing Musical Difficulty with Performance Quality,* I list ten factors to be aware of in relation to the rehearsal time available and number of shows performed:

1. Difficulty level of the music
2. Difficulty level of the drill
3. Length of pieces of music
4. Number of pieces of music
5. Number of drill sets to learn
6. Utilizing balance between rehearsing music and rehearsing drill
7. Amount of material to learn for the next performance
8. Amount of time until the next performance
9. Amount of time for sectionals
10. Amount of individual preparation outside rehearsal

These ten factors must be carefully weighed and evaluated in order to put the students in a position to succeed.

On the other end of the spectrum, bands such as Western Carolina and Arizona only perform one halftime show a year. This approach is modeled after DCI, where the goal is to perform one show at an extraordinarily high level and get as close to perfection as possible. The pinnacle for these bands each season is hosting their band festivals and performing in front of up to forty high school bands and band directors and hundreds of high school students they hope to recruit. At Western Carolina, percussion instructor Matt Henley explained their one show philosophy:

*Our number one goal is to prepare our music education majors for the real world as a high school band director. Since most high school band programs compete and only do one show, our students will be prepared for that. Our second goal is to give our music education majors and student coordinators and staff teaching and administration experience running a band program. Another important goal we have is to perfect a performance, achieve a high level of excellence and quality, and give the students a strong sense of accomplishment. We also found that our football crowd loves our show and they seem to appreciate the quality and enjoy seeing what new things have been added to the show each week. We also do one show to give the band what they want in terms of a very difficult musical book. Finally, we do it for recruiting. We host our contest, the Tournament of Champions, and also do exhibitions. The students in the band love [the show] and the crowd loves it too.*

When attending the Western Carolina football game, I noticed there were approximately 15,000 fans in attendance.

The Catamounts are not known as a football powerhouse, but they do have good fan support and a spirited football atmosphere. After the "Pride of the Mountains" performed at halftime, the engaged crowd gave them a standing ovation. As the band exited the field, I noticed a mass of people starting to leave. There couldn't have been more than 10,000 fans in the stands for the second half. All I could think about was how many people came to see and hear the band.

Many programs, like Alabama's Million Dollar Band, split the difference and perform three halftime shows a year, giving the fans and band members enough musical variety during the season while averaging 2-3 weeks to prepare a new show. This can make the rehearsal time a little more manageable, giving the students more time to learn, memorize, and clean their music and drill. It also gives these bands the opportunity to perform their shows more than once. Repeating shows, although frowned upon by some band programs, provides students the time to prepare and develop confidence. To paraphrase leadership expert and author John Maxwell, "You have to crockpot a piece of music, not microwave it."

## Competitive Auditions

Actor Kevin Coster once said in the popular movie, *Field of Dreams,* "If you build it, they will come." The best college marching bands and drumlines are considered the best because they have been successful building a culture and a program that students want to join. What attracts students the most is the quality of the product and the inspiration to say, "I want to be a part of that!"

Several of the drumlines I visited turn many students away each year. With so many good players trying out, these drumlines are never short on talent and do not have to worry about filling their instrumentation. In addition to the quality of the product, competitive auditions are also influenced by how large the undergraduate student population is and whether or not marching band is a requirement. The larger universities, such as Ohio State, Michigan State, Arizona, and LSU have a substantial talent pool to pick from but *do not* require music majors to march. Other schools like Alabama have a one-year marching band requirement for music majors, Western Carolina a two-year requirement, and North Texas a three-year requirement. For more information on undergraduate student population and marching band requirements at each school, see Chapter 9, *Crunching the Numbers.*

Competitive auditions become competitive when you are able to get better *people* and recruit better talent to your program. But another important part of achieving excellence as a band or drumline is the ability to develop the talent you already have, and get people *better*. Many schools achieve this through drumming classes, private lessons, help sessions, and camps during the summer. ▧

# CHAPTER 1

# Setting Goals

"Are you here for something to do, or are you here to do something?"—JEFF JANSSEN

In my experience, college marching bands usually attract two kinds of students—those who want something to do, and those who want to *do* something. The gap between these two mindsets is significant and can be seen in a student's commitment level and the goals they set for themselves. According to sports leadership expert Jeff Janssen, students who just want something to do have a commitment level that can be described as *compliant*. "Compliant people do what they are told by their coaches and team leaders, are obedient soldiers who do what is expected but lack the initiative to go above and beyond, do enough to maintain whatever standard is set by the leader but aren't willing to do any extra, and are frustrating to teach because the leaders always have to supply the direction and motivation."

In contrast, students who want to *do* something want to do something special and can be described as *compelled*. Janssen says compelled people "won't rest until they get the job done, prepare and practice at the highest level, never go through the motions, take advantage of every opportunity to get better, hold themselves and their teammates to a higher standard, and perform to their potential on a consistent basis." One of the secrets to success in a large organization like a marching band is to get more students who want to do something and less who just want something to do. In other words, more compelled–less compliant.

Setting goals for your organization is one of the most important steps on the road to achieving excellence. Goals inspire, challenge, stretch, motivate, and provide direction but will not gain any momentum without commitment. As Mack Douglas said, "The achievement of your goal is assured the moment you commit yourself to it."

My first interview question to the band directors and drumline instructors was, "What are your long term goals each season?" I was curious as to whether each band's goals were written down for students to see, or if they were just stated verbally. I also wanted to know if the drumline had additional goals for themselves as they started each season.

## The Golden Band from Tigerland

My first interview was with Frank Wickes, Director of Bands at LSU, approaching his 50th year as a band director and his 28th at LSU. "What we're trying to do is to maintain any standard we have set and to see to it that it stays up on the level that all of us expect and want it to be. We have a strong and rich tradition at LSU that goes back at least 45 years." Wickes goes on to say, "We want to keep the program in the public eye the way everybody's accustomed to seeing it and hopefully it can stay there and be a little bit better if possible."

The continuity of the LSU band staff has played a major role. "It has been very important to keep the staff together," said Wickes. "We have very good help. Linda Moorhouse, our Associate Director of Bands, is our secret weapon. She is a special drill writer and is really the secret to our success."

When asked about the band's goals, Moorhouse responded, "Our goal is to be better than we were the year before. Musically, I try to push the envelope collectively. A lot of these students have waited their whole lives to be in the Tiger Band. These students are treated like royalty on campus. It's a big deal if you're in the band."

The final piece of the puzzle is Assistant Director of Bands, Roy King. "We want to put a product on the field in front of the general public that is at least as good as the year before and hopefully better," King said. "We're constantly trying to make it better, or as good as we can make it." Graduate Assistant Ben Chamberlain added, "When it comes to our goals, I try and talk to the drumline about their role. The most important goal is to have them play music that helps the band and to have them prepared every week."

## Roll Tide!

At the University of Alabama, drumline instructor and arranger Neal Flum has built one of the top college drumlines in the country. Every aspect of the marching percussion ensemble is first-rate under his leadership from his top-shelf website to the caliber of players to his five-member percussion staff. According to Flum, "I would say that our long term goals are to provide a quality, constructive, and educational experience for the students. I would also tell you that one of our other long term goals is to continuously improve the performance level of the students and the teaching performance of the staff. We don't really measure ourselves against other groups because we don't really take a competitive mindset, so we hope that wherever we've started, that we've journeyed as far forward as we could. We want to improve our technique, our quality of sound, our musicianship, and the level of clarity of what we perform. We just want to get better and we want to do it in a way which educates them and allows them the opportunity to teach other people as well."

Alabama's 2007 Percussion Staff included Neal Flum, director, Michael Keeton, Tony Riddle, Colin Choat, and Marcus Bishop. Ken Ozzello, Director of the University of Alabama Million Dollar Band said of his goals for the band, "Our goal is to get better each year and really try to focus on improving the sound of the band. I try not letting the fact that it is a marching band adversely affect the sound of the group. We also use a marching style that allows the students to play their instruments without hindrance."

## Pride of the Mountains

At Western Carolina University, Director of Athletic Bands Bob Buckner has built a powerhouse program in the mountains of North Carolina. Now in his 20th year at WCU, Buckner sheds some light on his goals for the Pride of the Mountains Marching Band. "Our main goal is to give our students a really good experience. I want them to walk away saying I was part of a great organization, a great band. You are literally building memories, through significant events, both with the band and athletics, and these are things that are fun to remember somewhere down the road. That's probably our number one goal. We also want to make it a laboratory experience for our music education majors. We want to prepare our music education majors for the real world as a high school band director and make it a leadership opportunity for all who want to be involved."

Matt Henley, drumline instructor and Associate Director of Athletic Bands at WCU, says, "As far as the whole goes, I want them to have a good time. I think a lot of guys get too hung up on excellence over fun. I think you can have both. I firmly believe that. I think we're doing a pretty good job of achieving that each season. At the end of the year if they can have as much fun at the last game as they did at the first, I think we've achieved that."

## We are Spartans

Michigan State University's Spartan Marching Band has a long and distinguished history and tradition. Director of the

Spartan Band, John Madden, did not hesitate to talk about his goals for the 2007 season. "Our goal is to balance carefully all the things performers in ensembles need to do to be good ensembles—to balance the motivation to be a better player, a better marcher, a better ensemble member, and a better leader. All of that goal-oriented behavior would be no different than if we were in a concert band or a jazz band, or a symphony orchestra. Our goal is for the students to be good ensemble members."

Madden continues, "There is a long tradition of excellence at Michigan State. It's not a band that's casual in any way. When it's time to play, when it's time to tune, the approach, the effort to the approach to get that to happen at a high level is what the culture is all about. Then we balance it with—'Band is fun!' One of my favorite expressions here is 'This is just band.' Would you relax? Dial it back, take it down a notch. We try and get kids invested to be in a good ensemble, to work hard, to influence others around them to work hard so the product is of very high caliber."

Jon Weber, Michigan State's drumline instructor has built a drumline which reflects the rich heritage of excellence of the Michigan State Band. The drumline plays at a very high level and has developed a culture of hard work, discipline, dedication, and pride. Becoming a member of the drumline is in high demand, as Weber had to turn away forty players in 2007. When asked about his goals for the MSU Drumline, Weber said, "I guess the main goal is to have a group that plays very well together, gets along together, enjoys what they do, but achieves a high level of playing and excellence." He also makes it clear to them from the very beginning that, "the one thing we're all here to do is to be the best drumline we can possibly be. That comes before everything else."

## TBDBITL

At The Ohio State University, Jon Woods is the Director of the Ohio State University Marching Band. Without question, Ohio State's tradition is one of the strongest in the country. Their identity as a marching band in our current culture of band competitions, props, set design, electronics, and visual stimuli stands alone. What are the goals each season for "The Best Damn Band in the Land?" According to Woods, "Well, one of our long term goals is to be better than we were last year in every aspect. We analyze everything we do after the season is over—recruiting, marching, playing, arranging, music—nothing gets overlooked. This has been in place for years. The biggest tradition here is a tradition of excellence. I expect the band to be better when I'm gone. That tradition of excellence needs to be built upon. And it does work. Today [Wednesday of a one-week show] I'm not going to have to say much at all because our kids know what they have to get done and what the expectations are of their performance." Drumline instructor Gary Hodges adds of his drumline's goals, "We really don't talk about it. I have my own personal goals such as to upgrade the bass drum section (to a more contemporary tuning and playing style), and each year trying to increase the difficulty of the music to a certain level we can take the line to. More students now are willing to do that."

## The Aura of North Texas

At the University of North Texas, home of the largest College of Music in the country including 130 percussion majors in 2007, there is a unique history of having *two* drumlines. One of the reasons I selected North Texas as part of my research was to find out exactly how this works and how the percussion department manages two drumlines. I had the chance to interview Paul Rennick, instructor of UNT's Indoor Drumline A, and a leader in the marching percussion activity. Here's Rennick's explanation of how the two drumlines came into being:

> *Because we had so many percussionists at UNT and marching band was a 3-year requirement for music majors, we had two drumlines. The A-line was the top line and the B-line was the second line. Before 1995, both lines would play with the marching band, alternating shows and games. The A-line would play the first show, then start to work on the PASIC (Percussive Arts Society International Convention) show, while the B-line worked on the second show with the marching band. Eventually, the A-line became the indoor line exclusively and the B-line became the marching band line.*

Nick Williams, Director of the Green Brigade Marching Band at UNT said of his goals for the band, "With so many music education majors here, I want to give them another way to teach band and give them techniques to use. The music education part of it is definitely part of the goal-making process. At UNT, there has to be a certain level of challenging material, otherwise a mutiny might happen! I want them to have fun, be good, and understand what it is that we do here. Students know what they're expecting."

According to marching band drumline instructors Frank Nedley and Matt Filosa, "We want to give them as much information as they need to get the job done. We want them to be able to apply the information when they teach. I think that's a key aspect of what we try to do, especially since it's mostly music education majors in the drumline. It's important that we teach in a way that they can learn from not just musically, but in a teaching manner, and being able to apply that when they go out [and teach]. At North Texas, the A-line is the performing line. The B-line is learning how to actually teach the activity."

## Desert Pride

At the University of Arizona, Jay Rees is the Director of the Pride of Arizona. Hearing him speak about The Pride is like hearing a man on a mission, exhibiting determination, passion, and above all innovation in what they are trying to do and the message they are trying to communicate. What are Jay Rees' goals?

"The long term goal is the same every year. I want the band to experience several things. I want them to have an experience that is meaningful to them as a future professional, whatever that is. I want them to have an experience that is something that can inform themselves as a young adult, as a young professional forever. I want to create an environment where they can have success in performing arts. I've always felt that success in the performing arts is a great window into personal human success on a lot of levels—professionally, personally, interpersonally. We're in the business of making better people. It's really that simple."

"But there's more to it than that. I want the kids to think about *why* that's happening. I don't just want to do it *to* them. I want them to recognize that they're going through a potentially transformative experience that is helping them be more focused, more dedicated, more conscientious, more responsible, more accountable, more passionate, more caring, more open, more artistic, and more sensitive. I want them to recognize that that's what they're having because if they own that, that's when something really does happen. I can't do that *to* them. I can provide the environment, I can provide the culture, I can provide the material and I can ride you until you either decide to step up or decide this isn't for you. And both of those realizations are good and valuable in some way. I can do all those things, but I can't make you have a significant life experience that informs who you are, but my goal is certainly to provide an environment where that can take place."

When asking the Arizona drumline instructors about their goals for the season, Saul Aguilar and Vicente Lopez said, "We have an experienced line this year. We knew cleanliness and rhythmic accuracy factors would be there. Our biggest goal was to instill some musicality and along with that evolve the technique program. In the beginning we had an evolution to get the rhythmic accuracy and rhythmic clarity. Now we're still in the process of getting what we do a little more musical so it's not a stereotypical drumline. We're also trying to get a very consistent sound from everybody." ◼

# CHAPTER 2

# Establishing Expectations

---

"Perform at your best by choice, not by chance."—GARY MACK

---

One common characteristic of all excellent organizations is the communication of clear expectations. In a college marching band setting, these expectations are often found in the course syllabus or band handbook presented to the members at the beginning of the season. These expectations are clearly communicated to the band members at the very first meeting or rehearsal each year, setting the tone for the entire season. Without question, buying into, meeting, and exceeding these expectations are the keys to success for every band program.

Band members are unique in that they are accountable for their actions on and off the field, as they serve as ambassadors of the university and often represent the largest student organization on campus. All the bands I observed establish high standards and expectations for its members, but it is important to note that these standards and expectations do not just appear in the band handbook, they are embedded in each band's culture. Furthermore, the message of establishing expectations comes not only from the band director, but the band staff and student leaders as well. In other words, expectations are established by a leadership *team*. A marching band's expectations can cover a wide range of issues from absences to travel policies to memorizing music. But most of the expectations, such as being a team player, treating others with respect, and having a positive attitude can be found in other high-performance organizations as well, further emphasizing the value of the marching band experience.

## Great Expectations

LSU's Linda Moorhouse was very clear in her thoughts on what is expected of all Tiger Band members. She addressed areas ranging from the band's visibility to rehearsal behavior. "Tiger Band is the biggest public relations vehicle that LSU has," says Moorhouse. "Everything they do is reflected all the way to the top of LSU. Our expectations are that they conform to what we want them to do in terms of uniforms, hair length, attitudes, or behavior in the stands. As far as rehearsals, I'm a big believer in giving ownership to the bandsmen. The more they take ownership, the more that all those internal things are controlled. As far as the collective behavior on the field, it needs to be in an orderly fashion."

Assistant Director of Bands Roy King focused on musical expectations in addition to a change in the type of students joining the band. "We want them to leave the semester being better performers on their instrument. Better musicians. Raised admissions standards on campus have resulted in a somewhat different type of student. Kids are more serious about their grades, coursework, and their degree pursuit."

Graduate Assistant Ben Chamberlain discussed his expectations for the drumline and consequences for not meeting them. "This year, our expectations are pretty lofty. The music has to be memorized by Thursday. If they get all of their music on Monday, then it must be memorized by Thursday's rehearsal. If they do that, they can play their warm-up on the hill on game day, which is kind of a tradition. If it's not memorized, we don't go do the hill as a group. It's not about individuals, it's about the group."

When asking the LSU section leaders what they expect from their fellow drumline members, Jeremy Logan replied, "We expect a good grasp of the fundamentals and the ability to play clean fast, especially since we learn a new show every week with the little amount of rehearsal we get every day. Timing is also important, as well as a good attitude. Over the last two years, this is probably the closest the drumline has ever been as far as attitude. We all get along. If there's a problem, it gets resolved pretty quickly."

Assistant section leader Tommy Bowen comments, "The drumline needs to see the need for all the things we do. This is a new ballgame. This is not your high school. You need to step it up and you need to memorize. Don't come to rehearsal still learning your music. We expect them to have a good time. In the past the attitude of the drumline has sometimes been apathetic. At the end of last year, and definitely this year, the attitude on the line is completely different. We're starting to learn, especially with Ben [our instructor] being here, what is good and what is not."

Throughout the history of the LSU Drumline, undergraduate student leadership has been a constant. On occasion, as in 2007, they have had a graduate assistant instructing them. To their credit, the LSU Drumline continues to raise its expectations each year and has developed into a talented, dedicated, and cohesive unit.

One would never know that behind the great tradition, high standards, and outstanding leadership at LSU are the day to day challenges facing them in terms of facilities. The LSU band room, which opened in 1959, has never been renovated and was originally built for a band of 140. Today the band stands at 325. Due to lack of space, the marching band does not have any indoor rehearsals and many band members cannot watch the pregame and halftime videos in the band room for the same reason. According to Robin Miller in an article she wrote in December 2007, "We don't go into the band room at all now," [Roy] King said. "Only our three concert groups use it, and it's not even big enough for them. The Tiger Band always rehearses outside. Rain or shine, we're out there."

King goes on to say in the article, "I think the Tiger Band is a victim of its own success. People see the glitz and glamour on Saturday nights, and they see a successful program. It's working, so if it's not broken, don't fix it...they see only the results of a major college marching band program but nothing behind the scenes."

It is a credit to the leadership of Frank Wickes, Linda Moorhouse, and Roy King for building and maintaining one of the top college marching bands in the country. So how do they do it? As someone who saw their facilities firsthand, I can say with confidence it is because of the kind of people they are and the expectations they set for their program. Students want to play for them. They want to be part of the great tradition of the Golden Band of Tigerland. At the time of this writing, a massive fundraising effort is successfully taking place to build a new band hall at LSU. When you have good people, excellent leaders, and high expectations, you find a way to succeed.

## Million Dollar Expectations

Upon arriving in Tuscaloosa, it was evident the University of Alabama Drumline had high expectations. From the way they approached the instruments, to the intensity of the staff, to the culture surrounding rehearsal, this drumline played and rehearsed at a very high level.

"Unfortunately my expectations are unrealistic," says Neal Flum, director of the Alabama Drumline. "I expect them to be as passionate, committed, and work as hard as I do, and that's not always the case. I expect them to come to rehearsal prepared. I expect them to perform at the level which we set for them, in terms of having their materials, their rehearsal etiquette, their practice time away from the ensemble, and how they engage their performances. Quite frankly we expect the highest level from them that we can possible set because they're not only learning to drum, they're developing life skills and setting themselves up for life beyond school. I think they benefit from a high level of expectation in both their performance and what they'll do outside the university when they go on to other things."

In regards to the conduct expected as members of the Million Dollar Band, Flum says, "I expect them to act like ladies and gentlemen. I expect them to be appreciative and respectful. We tell them they should never criticize another group. They should be respectful of what other people do and try and learn from those groups and individuals."

Alabama band director Ken Ozzello expects his band members to be model examples for the university. "We are constantly preaching to them that they are not in the general population, and that they are absolutely representing the university," says Ozzello. "The university has invested an incredible amount of time and all the people who have been in the program before are counting on them to represent the group and university. We're really looking for model behavior to make the university proud."

## Elevated Expectations

Western Carolina's Pride of the Mountains members also demonstrate high expectations in everything they do. Bob Buckner summed it up in one word—Responsibility! "Sometimes the students have adult bodies, but not adult maturity," Buckner says. "We're very big on that. I trust them, but I want them to understand that when they go out into the real world, someone's going to expect that accountability. They've learned that here. I think that's the big thing. I want them to work hard. I'm disappointed if I don't feel like we get their best effort. At rehearsal yesterday it wasn't that they didn't work hard, it's just that they weren't focused. That's a matter of maturity for the band. Our shows cannot be done on auto-pilot. They'll hurt themselves and others!"

When asked about the drumline's expectations, WCU instructor Matt Henley focused on being realistic as well as bringing out the best in his students. "I don't get into big time specifics with individual stuff. I do not tell them, 'I expect you to practice an hour on your own every day.' I think that's ludicrous to expect that with college kids' schedules today. I think if you are realistic, then every time they're not behind the drums they're [with their] friends and they have a good time. Then when they are behind a drum, they're expected to show up with their game face on, and they're expected to have a certain level of excellence every time they strap on a drum. That is a mentality that will take them outside of a drumline...anytime they show up to do a gig, they'll bring that level of professionalism."

I also spent some time with WCU's front ensemble. With such a strong emphasis on electronics in the Pride of the Mountains halftime show, the front ensemble plays a significant role and over the last few years has steadily become a very competitive section in its own right. How has the front ensemble developed into such a high-performing unit? They raised their expectations. "We just decided, we're going to make it good," said Henley. "It's all about expectations and accountability, just like anything you want to be good. We took the nucleus of the players we had, started trying to instruct them outside of marching band to get them to another level, and then we really started trying to hardcore recruit some fantastic mallet players by doing home visits, phone calls, cards, you name it, and we ended up getting some killer players. This year, every one of those kids can really play!"

"As far as rehearsal discipline," Henley says, "occasionally the band is not centered, especially when adding choreography to the show. The band might get a little loud, talkative, or a little social. This year's band is pretty young—including 172 freshmen—and with that comes its own challenges with maturity. Other than that, I've rarely had a discipline problem. Well, I take that back! The only time I ever had a discipline problem was two years ago. I had a cymbal player who had an attitude. I was not use to having that at all, so we just invited him to leave. He showed up the next day, apologized to me, the cymbal line, the percussion section, and he never opened his mouth the rest of the season."

The WCU section leaders have their own expectations and emphasize good attitudes, the persona of being a drummer, and having a chip on their shoulder. Tenor captain Grady Wiley says, "Walk in and demand yourself to be better than everybody else. As a line, we've always had the idea of being able to turn it on. When it's time to turn it on you've got to turn on that professionalism and say, hey, this is what we're going to do and it's time to get down to business."

Bass drum section leader Brian Dumas expects his section to understand the basics of being able to read music and having some sort of technique to work off of. "Struggling through band camp is what it's all about," said Brian. "Barely making it, having sunburn everyday; knowing you have to come early the next day to tune your drum to get ready, it just sets you up for the season to be on task."

Section leader Scott Lanning added, "I think we're uptight at times. We have a lot of fun, but we're pretty uptight at times. It's a good thing when it comes to pushing people that want to be better and when they're not doing their best."

## Passing it Down

At Michigan State, band director John Madden emphasizes how important it is for the students who have been through the program to pass down expectations. Madden went on to state plainly, that the attitude of the MSU band is, "If you're going to do it, do it right. My vigilance to us is being classy, behaving well, being good citizens, and knowing that we have a responsibility because we wear a uniform with the insignia of the university. We're a lot like athletes in terms of representing the university. We kind of live the high-profile band member life. When someone acts out of line, we say 'That's not who we are, that's not what we do.' That's what we're about, or that's not what we're about. Our expectations are part of the culture. Rehearsal starts the same way every day. I think we are probably as disciplined in rehearsal as anybody as far as being on task, disciplined, on pace, and the effectiveness of what we do. I would like for anybody to come observe the band and watch any minute of any rehearsal—old show, new show—and have their impression be, 'this is organized and this is disciplined, and the kids know how to rehearse."

One of Madden's philosophies is called, "Cross the white lines", which means "Once you step over the [side] line at 4:30 (the start of practice), don't bring into the equation your engineering mid-term or your personal relationships—just have a good time."

"The other piece to this," says Madden, "is to keep it balanced and have fun, be a Spartan fan, and support your team. We don't have the option to let our emotions change with losing. We're attached to the team, like any college band is [and as far as winning and losing], Michigan State is like the Chicago Cubs. He continues, "MSU is a school associated with a big tradition and an identity. We definitely have a culture of student leaders and veteran members passing down to younger members our routine. It's a real 'pass-it-down' band. This is how we do this. We wear our band jacket like this. We don't do this."

According to drumline instructor Jon Weber, the MSU Drumline has very high expectations. "Performance-wise, I expect that they're able to do everything that I throw at them. The halftime shows have to be at a very high level. I would expect it to be similar to a drum corps as the final product; obviously there's a lot more music, so there's the learning curve and all that, but when it's performed it should be at a very high level. And then, I expect them to be classy representatives of Michigan State University and I expect they will be good citizens of the band and the drumline. As far as attitudes, I think that working together, valuing each person's role to the success of the line, and putting the group ahead of themselves are all done a lot within the group; it's just something that I expect. And if a problem ever happened, it would probably be just an isolated case and not happen very often at all."

MSU tenor captain Mark Racalla says, "Probably one of the big things for us on game days is preparation - knowing your music." Cymbal captain Mike Irwin adds, "One of our expectations is being able to perform on your own—being able to do it by yourself. You don't want to be pulled around the field. Music memorization is expected." Bass drum captain Dimetrious White commented, "Do your best. If you do mess up, just try to get right back into it. Nobody's perfect." Section leader Jordan Novak shared a mature perspective. "Expectations change depending on what we're doing. There is a different amount of detail and different level of execution, depending on how much rehearsal time we have. With six different halftime shows, we have to go back to square one each week. Expectations also depend on how many new members we have. We're really young this year and have a lot of new guys."

## Expect Tradition

At Ohio State, Jon Woods says that rehearsal discipline is the key to everything. "That is primary. There's a lot of student ownership in the band. That ownership, in the final analysis, takes us to another level. I think that we have a good system where it follows a chain of command. It's a military tradition, following a hierarchy. When you're a freshman, you look and listen. When you're a sophomore, you learn some more. By the time you're in your 3rd year, the payback starts, which means it's time that you start teaching the new people the fundamentals—discipline, standards, goals, what's expected, how well you should play, etc."

Another important expectation critical to the OSU band's success is having music memorization checks on Friday before each home game. "The standard of music is very high. We memorize all of our music. There's a difference between the band on Thursday and the band on Friday. The whole thing goes to another level. If they fail their music check, they are out of the band for the following week. It's taken years to get the level to where it is. Then there is an appeal process. If they fail their music check by their squad leader, they can play it again for one of the directors. This gives them a second chance, but we want to support our squad leaders. I think we're really going to get to that next level when somebody fails a music check because they didn't play all the dynamics, or phrased where they were supposed to. It's more than just pushing down the valves and getting the notes and the rhythms right, especially if you're repeating a show. It should go up another level."

Percussion instructor Gary Hodges adds, "I expect them to come prepared and know their music outside of rehearsal. Every rehearsal they come to, they should leave feeling they can do something better. Legendary Ohio State football coach Woody Hayes said, 'You're either getting better or getting worse. You're never staying the same." Hodges adopts that philosophy. "Think ahead," he says. "Work outside so we're not spinning our wheels." As far as performing at a high level, the Ohio State Drumline expects it of themselves. "It's there from the history of the program," says Hodges, "all because of the competitiveness of making it. They know what's expected of them and they come in and do it."

The Ohio State Drumline section leaders had a lot to say about this issue of expectations. According to assistant section leader Scott Pethuyne, "There's always a lot to expect. March to the best of your abilities, learn your music, and be with it on the field. Everybody knows this about practice. Everybody knows what is expected, what the band does. Day in and day out, it's a matter of how mentally involved you are. That's the expectation and that's the challenge."

Section leader Amanda White says, "Focus and consistency at each rehearsal are big. We know everybody's busy with classes, homework, exams, and stuff you have to get ready for. It's nice when you come to rehearsal and let everything else go to the side. Just focus on music, marching, and making the band and your sections better. I expect my section to come in ready to work for those two hours—not leaps and bounds over—but I definitely expect the same amount of work and focus from everyone so we can keep the section consistent and sounding good throughout the entire week."

Scott agrees. "The biggest thing we can do is to focus in on what we're doing at that point and focus on doing it well, rather than thinking about all the other things and music that get thrown at us. We work really hard to be in band here. It's pretty prestigious and not very many people get the opportunity to be a part of our band. So I want to memorize my music early, learn my drill well, and make the most out of the opportunities I get and try not to take for granted the fact that I get to come here. Sometimes you get into a rut and think about the hundreds of kids that would love to come to a rehearsal and memorize some tough music. I try not letting the section forget that they are in a privileged position and we have a responsibility and a job to do also. It's a privilege, not a right."

Tenor section leader Justin Argentine raises a great point. "We live in an organization that calls itself TBDBITL—The Best Damn Band in the Land. And regardless of whether we like the show or how we've been working, that's always the name. The expectation we try to convey is that we need to live up to that and not take it for granted."

Amanda adds some insight on musical difficulty. "If it's not hard, you should be able to play it perfectly. If we can't even play the easy stuff clean, how are we going to play this awesome solo clean? Even though we have some stuff that's not terribly difficult, I would hope that people would spend just as much time on that so it will all come together and it will be more fun."

## Tex-pectations

When asked about his expectations, UNT's Nick Williams focused mainly on preparation. "They do one sectional per week. By Friday before each performance, the music is memorized. Section leaders take on a lot of responsibility making sure their sections are getting their music learned. Every now and then, graduate students will do a random test. As far as behavior, some days are real relaxed. Others, I make it clear in the beginning that we're going to work. 90% of the time they're on task."

## Pride in Expectations

The Pride of Arizona is more than a fancy name for a college band. In the case of the University of Arizona Marching Band, the name defines and reflects what actually takes place on the practice field in terms of work ethic, rehearsal discipline, and pride in performance. Jay Rees explains: "I think one of the things that makes our program effective is that I think we're a model for rehearsal etiquette. One of the things that I'm very proud of and one of the things that the students pride themselves on is that we are effective in rehearsals. Everyone across the board understands what work ethic means and what rehearsal etiquette is and what good rehearsal etiquette is and what bad rehearsal etiquette is."

"There is a very high expectation for a quiet, focused learning atmosphere where nobody moves at attention, so when I say something, everybody's going to hear it," says Rees. "There's very, very, *very* little screwing around. At the same time, I think the band has fun. We make jokes, we laugh, they'll tease each other; there's times when you run it back to the form or run resetting something; of course there's going to be a little loosening up and that's fine. I think the thing that makes it work is they know when it's time."

Rees also has a very inspiring outlook towards improving throughout the season. "There's an expectation that we're going to get better as the year goes on. I'm not sure that a lot of bands do it that way. I think a lot of bands think, 'well, this is what we do and we'll do it some more next month, and we'll do it some more the month after that.' I tell them we should get better at learning material, learn things more efficiently and effectively, we should be better at things the second time we try them instead of the fifth time; our technique should be better which allows us to have success sooner. We are going to continue to improve the things that make us successful; marching technique, playing technique, articulation, rhythmic accuracy, style, as well as basic classroom discipline."

"In terms of expectations outside of rehearsal, we actually give them playing/memorization tests. They may start in the middle of a tune, and include mark time and halts, as it relates to drill moves. The whole body is incorporated into the playing tests. We make a big deal out of that—that memorizing a piece for performance is not 'I know my part.' "That's not it – then you don't! If all you know is your part, you don't."

"The other expectation is that the student leaders are expected to run at least one sectional outside of class per week. And *all* of them run more than that. The expectation is at least one—there absolutely has to be one a week. If there are class conflicts, the section leaders will hold two sectionals during the week in order to accommodate everybody's schedule. If you can make both, you make both and if you can only make one or the other, at least you were at one sectional per week. Sectionals usually last between 30-45 minutes and usually take place before or after rehearsal." Rees impresses upon his band that, "If you want to be really good, you have to have sectionals *all the time*. I mean, can you think of a time when there's nothing else to work on?"

When asked about the drumline's expectations, section leaders Saul Aguilar and Vicente Lopez added, "Expectations for everybody is to come out and be professional at all times. Obviously there's room for joking around. You have to have a balance there, but when we hear it affecting their playing, we'll immediately get on them. The music comes first—the music is always first. Whether it's a visual or attitude problems, the music always comes first. The other thing with these guys is that they're so close together hanging out all the time, so when they get out on the field, they sometimes have a hard time separating that." ◼

# CHAPTER 3

# Teaching Life Lessons

---

"You don't get to choose when to be great."
—NICK WILLIAMS

---

s I mentioned in the Introduction, I have always be-lieved that the marching band experience goes beyond band and even beyond music and can be used as a vehicle to teach life lessons such as hard work, preparation, confidence, consistency, commitment, attitude, leadership, teamwork, and focus. These lessons can either be consciously empha-sized during the season or easily taken for granted. According to sports coach and author Bruce Brown, "The profession of coaching is an awesome privilege and responsibility. A quality [athletic] experience should make a significant con-tribution to the lives of the individual participants...coaches cannot make the assumption that simply being part of an [athletic] experience will ensure that the participants will learn these lessons. Like anything else we hope to accomplish in our sport, we must plan for it, and teach it if we want it to happen."

One of my favorite interview questions to ask was, "What life lessons do you emphasize the most?" I was pleasantly surprised at the responses I received from everyone on this topic. It is obvious that the top college marching bands and the people leading them have thought a great deal about teaching their students values that transcend the activity itself.

## Wearing the Purple and Gold

When asked what values and life lessons he emphasized the most with the LSU Tiger Band, Frank Wickes looked me straight in the eye and enthusiastically exclaimed, "Good citizenship! The academic standards have been raised at LSU, so the type of kid has changed. LSU has good citizens. If we have problems, they're not behavioral. We have clear cut rules, but not a whole lot of them; mostly about game conduct and trip conduct and the uniform. But we do have citizenship rules." Wickes also stresses the importance of preparation. "As players, we expect the students to play, to be prepared and march their spot, and represent the university with the highest possible standards."

Roy King emphasizes the importance of teamwork in the band. "We try to impress upon them that it's a team effort, a group effort. It's not about the individual. That's the most important life lesson. That's a life lesson that will pay dividends for them later in life." When asked what he does when there is a student who doesn't buy into the team-first philosophy, King replied, "They're counseled. A student will act a certain way when they know they're being watched for a position in the band."

Linda Moorhouse shared with me the drumline's unique situation at LSU. "This year is one of the first years where we have had a graduate assistant overseeing the drumline. For the most part, the drumline is student run, but Ben Chamberlain has been able to gain the respect of the students and their friendship. He wants to take them to another level."

"I try to teach them that being good is fun," says Chamberlain. "Instruction needs to be engaging and energetic but focused, and has to be based on improvement. If members are working hard and they see results that work, then I think that's fun. That's really my entire value system. We're not here to show-off, we're here to help the band. It's similar to a drumset player in a band."

## Sweet Home Alabama

"I emphasize discipline and work ethic," says Neal Flum. "If you have a good work ethic and a good sense of self-discipline, those qualities will go a long way for you in the percussion section and elsewhere." Band director Ken Ozzello adds, "I believe the students have to be good representatives to the university and entertaining to the people that are watching."

## Mountainous Lessons

At Western Carolina, Bob Buckner has put a lot of thought into the experience he wants his band members to have. "I want them to be trustworthy. I want them to be the kind of people that can be counted on. I talk a lot about it, but I don't try to give them long lectures, but every day at the end of rehearsal I'll try to touch on maybe one point, kind of a thought for the day, maybe something that's come to my attention that I feel like they're not going to hear in an English class or a math class. The other thing that we talk a lot about is teamwork. It's realizing that we just simply can't function as individuals. You go to any other class, and it's you and the professor, but you go to our class, and it's you and everybody on the field. And in reality, isn't that life? People that are successful learn to play well with others. And I think that's what we try to get across to them."

Buckner continues, "A lot of that goes back to our student leaders. We can trace our retention rates to our section leaders. If we go into a situation where a section leader has been ineffective for one reason or another, maybe not competent, maybe the kids didn't respect that person, then the next year that number will be down."

Within the drumline, Matt Henley talks a lot about pulling your weight, and that you're only as strong as your weakest link. "We talk about the importance of having a team, and being there for your fellow teammates," says Henley. "We talk about education. Several guys in the line are education majors, and those that are not want to teach drumlines, so we use it as a teaching opportunity. I try to make them aware of why we do things. There's a lot of dialog that happens like that off the field."

## Spartan Values

Standing among the Michigan State band after their morning rehearsal on game day, I noticed several band members wearing their 2007 band t-shirts. On the back it read, "In the end, a Spartan's true strength is the warrior next to him." This seemed to sum up what I observed all week in East Lansing— a true pride and commitment to the values of the Michigan State band. When asked about the lessons he emphasizes to his students, John Madden had much to say.

"Any college marching band is the best life skills class on campus. The ultimate, bar none, above any other skill I emphasize is our band operates in an atmosphere of respect. After twenty-one years teaching college marching band, I have learned that the person at the top has to insert character and behavior expectations, along with musical and visual expectations. The latter is pretty easy—play well and march well. But behave well and treat each other with respect, that's much harder, 'roll-up-your sleeves' kind of work. That's really in the long run much more valuable."

Madden continues, "When we're in our rocking chairs, we're not going to be talking about that arrangement of *Malaguena*. We're talking about the personalities, the friendships, the leadership, and the directors who said 'let me know if I can ever do anything for you.' That's the key for me. Everybody in the band doesn't have to be everybody's buddy, everybody's best friend, but if we operate in an atmosphere of respect, everything else will fit into place."

"As far as life lessons," states drumline instructor Jon Weber, "the one I talk to them most about is preparation because that is what is on a day to day basis. I'd say commitment is also a big deal. I used to do more of this. I tried to mix in life lessons into the teaching. Maybe I should do more."

## Talkin' Trash

Some may be interested to discover that the Ohio State Band Center is actually located *in* Ohio Stadium. Enter Gate 10, walk up a flight of stairs, and you will notice a giant mural painted in tribute to the Ohio State Marching Band. Walking by the stadium one day on my way to the band center, I noticed an assortment of stadium trash cans sending a message and defining the culture on this campus: **Tradition, Excellence, Integrity, Innovation, Enrichment, and Respect.** I found this very intriguing and admired Ohio State's vision for all to see, even on the receptacles used during the football games.

The life lessons taught in the Ohio State Marching Band were many, and band director Jon Woods is at the forefront in terms of what he tries to teach his band members. "We try and teach them what you can accomplish with hard work, a team effort, and when everybody depends on everybody to have a successful performance. We emphasize commitment, perseverance, teamwork, working together, teaching, problem solving, working with people, and dedication." Woods points out that 75% of the band are non-majors, with 25% being music majors. He acknowledges that band members are the best and brightest kids in the university. "If you can get people in your job to function as efficiently as the band does, you'd have a winner!"

Gary Hodges mentioned leadership as one of the key life lessons he imparts on the OSU Drumline. "We talk a little bit about leadership and how to lead and the fact that leaders don't have to do all the work. To me a good leader incorporates the talents and abilities of everybody else, which makes them feel part of the package. For example, asking them to do some of the tuning, keeping the band room clean, or asking a freshman to write in the sticking for the show. How hard is that person going to work now that they own part of the show? A leader delegates and utilizes the talents of others. It doesn't matter who gets the credit."

Hodges continues, "Another example is if you're doing a sectional and you go around and there's a drag figure that somebody's interpreting better than you are, go ahead and set that as the one you're going to mimic. Whoever can do it the best. It can be a first year, a fourth year, or a fifth year member. It could be the squad leader. Again, how important is that person going to feel when they walk out of that room and how hard are they going to work? If you get everybody to feel that that the line is going to perform because of *them*, each and every individual will work hard. Delegating and getting to the point where everyone feels that there's ownership in that section and in that show is something that makes the whole line better."

## A Texas Education

At North Texas, band director Nick Williams says, "The things that we talk about all the time are do the right thing even though no one's watching, and respecting each other, the process, and everyone who's involved in the process. The other thing is work ethic. I've noticed that younger people don't have the same work ethic that I was raised with."

One of Williams' favorite quotes is, "You don't get to choose when to be great." This goes to consistency and coming to practice every day ready to work and ready to improve. Sometimes students make a decision not to work hard, for whatever reason. "If you do that in the real world," says Williams, "you get fired. If you don't get fired, you don't get raises or you don't get promotions." Williams uses the term "character flaws" a lot to describe students lacking this kind of self-discipline. Other life lessons he feels are important are how you talk to people and how you respond to people.

## Beyond Band

What life lessons does Arizona band director Jay Rees talk about with his band? "I think there are two parts to that," says Rees. "There's the experience of the season and the experience of being in this program. There are also the lessons of the art. The music we actually program can say something and mean something and teach something too. There are too many [bands] out there saying, let's play *Malaguena* again! Let's play *Sing Sing Sing.* Let's play *Louie Louie*! *Peanut Vendor* anyone?"

"If you're going to pull it out of the case, and put an instrument on your face or pick up a pair of sticks, it has to mean something. If it doesn't mean something why are you doing it? Just because it's marching band and just because the majority of the performances are at football games does not in my mind in any way negate the fact that the music can mean something. I consciously pick music for many different reasons, but one of them is that it has some message that speaks to me that I feel that I can work with during the season."

"The life lessons of being in the band—I think we all know what those are—it's about accountability, responsibility, dedication, focus, and passion. If you're not passionate about what you do, do something else! Those are the big lessons of being in the process. Students understand personal accountability better because they marched in the Pride of Arizona. They are more passionate about what they do. They believe in themselves and believe in the power of focus and commitment and they see that there's a payoff to being focused and committed."

# CHAPTER 4

# Studying Leadership Styles

"A team should be an extension of the coach's personality. My teams were arrogant and obnoxious."—AL MCGUIRE

As an avid sports fan during my travels, I couldn't help but notice some of the great coaches on each campus: Les Miles at LSU, Nick Saban at Alabama, Tom Izzo at Michigan State, Jim Tressel at Ohio State, and Lute Olsen at Arizona. Beyond these present-day coaches lay the aura and mystic of two coaching legends in particular—Woody Hayes at Ohio State and Paul "Bear" Bryant at Alabama. In fact, my hotel in Tuscaloosa was located right next door to the Bear Bryant Museum, a living tribute to the legendary Alabama leader.

While college football and college band certainly have more differences than similarities, I had the opportunity to observe and study the leadership styles of the band directors and drumline instructors and watch them do what they do on their home turf. I learned how they communicate and connect with their students, and how their students respond to their leadership. According to sports psychologist and author H.A. Dorfman, "Different [coaches] will have different styles; they can all be effective...I would often remind myself that I wasn't coaching 'a sport,' but coaching young people who were playing a sport...To a great extent, our leadership style is not what we think it is—but what the players think it is."

## Setting the Bar

When describing his leadership style with the Tiger Band, LSU's Frank Wickes says it's important to put the ownership on the students. "Having them take ownership in the band and exhibit the pride that they feel as leaders and as returning members is what we want them to experience," explains Wickes. "We want them to raise the standards of that citizenship and make everybody responsible for their preparation and for their actions, and to wear the uniform with pride. The student leadership is pretty special here."

Linda Moorhouse's comments were more specific to her rehearsal style. "I think it depends on the day," says Moorhouse. "I want to make Tiger Band fun, but at the same time, to keep the pace going very fast in rehearsal. The students either learn to catch up and stay with me, or they're the ones who lag behind and they'll be on the sideline the next week."

## Role Model Leadership

Neal Flum's leadership style has been shaped and influenced by DCI Hall of Famer Thom Hannum, Associate Director of Bands and Percussion Instructor at the University of Massachusetts. Flum explains, "In keeping with Thom Hannum's work at UMASS, the big thing we focus on at Alabama is 'Role Model Leadership.' You don't really need to say anything. You don't really need to ask anything. You just need to perform in a manner that is an excellent example, hoping that they'll follow that example. Role Model Leadership includes being on time, working hard, and exhibiting passion, commitment, and respect. If I succeed at those things, I expect my students to do the same. We try to lay out the structure of rules and regulations in our handbook. We require our students to sign off that they have read and understand the handbook. We put a lot of responsibility on the students. It is a very collaborative process and we have a great staff."

## Be Consistent

After almost 20 years as Director of the Pride of the Mountains, Bob Buckner was almost caught off guard by the question. "My style? There are probably people who would take issue with it! I think I lead by example. I work really hard, I love the band, I graduated here, and I love the university." I've always been one of those people that if you're going to compete, compete at the highest level, that way at least somebody good will beat you!"

WCU Percussion Instructor Matt Henley says, "My leadership style is consistency. They know exactly how I'm going to be that day. I think that's so important. There are so many instructors that I know that are not that way, and that just inhibits the learning process. I try and be upbeat, I try to kid with my kids. We take what we do seriously, but when it's time to relax we'll still try and have a good time. I think with older kids, they truly appreciate that, but when it is time to work, I always hold them accountable—always!"

## Spheres of Influence

Michigan State band director John Madden also emphasizes consistency. "There are not a lot of highs, not a lot of lows. I'm very much on the positive, optimistic side of things. I may be a little more relentless of the pursuit of the details if time allows than sometimes the group expects. And what I've learned over the years is that's what they want."

"At our leadership workshop, we talk about the 'Spheres of Influence.' There are three spheres—what I can control, what I can influence, and what I cannot control or influence. If you ask a Spartan Marching Band member, 'what can you control?' the answers you will get are my uniform, my level of preparation, and my attitude. What can you influence? Answers are the person next to me, or running back to my spot. What can't you control? It's 50 degrees today, that we've lost 2 big ten games, the rehearsal schedule, or the condition of the field."

Percussion Instructor Jon Weber states, "I try to be an example of what I would expect them to be in a similar situation. A lot of the students will hopefully be in a teaching situation in these sorts of groups, and most of them end up doing it whether it's in the summer or later on in life. I tell them they teach me how to teach them. It's definitely a reciprocal relationship and we achieve it together. The section leaders are a huge part of what we do. It's kind of the mantra of the Spartan Marching Band; having levels of command in the group."

## Behind the Horn

Ohio State band director Jon Woods says his leadership style is quiet but effective; firm but fair. "I try to be consistent with how I handle the discipline and with what I expect on the podium and on the field. It's interesting how we evolve. When I was a band director in my youth in 1968, I was from the "K. A." school of band directors; you think of Patton, you think of Woody Hayes, that leadership kind of era. Do what I say. Shut up and sit down. We're not into that these days. I went through those years of operating very successfully. At some point in time, you notice that person behind the horn; that there's a human being behind the horn. My teaching style evolved to what it is today.

Gary Hodges describes his style as being "non-demonstrative." "I say very little to the section if things are going well," says Hodges. "When things are not going well, I start having meetings and hanging around the section more. There are some non-verbal things that I do and some verbal. We'll discuss where we're going, what we want to do, and then we look back on the season and ask whether or not we accomplished to our full abilities or did we spin our wheels and waste some time? I try to lead low key based on situational need. The more I'm not involved then they know that things are going OK."

## Spectacular and Unacceptable

"My leadership style," states Jay Rees, "is what it is. I think I lead by example in the sense that I'm extremely intense, extremely passionate about what we're doing, intensely focused, and there's no grey area with me. There's spectacular and there's unacceptable. There's only two—there's only two ways to do things."

Rees continues, "My biggest job is to show up to every rehearsal and be the most focused, intense, driven, passionate person I can be and hopefully that will rub off, and it does! They know and they want that! They'll get disappointed if I don't. It's just about caring and being really passionate. I think the other key to my leadership style is organization and efficiency. I want my kids to know, and completely trust that they're going to come to every rehearsal and it's going to be efficient and effective and worth their time. The only way that happens is if I'm totally prepared and the staff is totally prepared. Everybody's on the same page and everybody's sending the same message about what we're doing and why." Ⓜ

# CHAPTER 5

# Instilling Motivation

"Motivation gets you going, habits get you there."—JOHN MAXWELL

For years I have been fascinated with the balance between intrinsic and extrinsic motivation within the marching band activity. In many high school programs, band is a competitive activity, offering external motivators such as ratings, rankings, scores, judges' tapes, and trophies to reward winning. In contrast, college band is based on entertainment rather than competition, teaching students to develop intrinsic motivation and values such as accountability, self-discipline, and pride.

According to my article, *Teaching the Values of Competition*:

*Unfortunately, marching band is often treated as an Olympic sport, and winning becomes the ultimate goal. One of the most alarming trends I've noticed is students becoming conditioned to respond only to motivation associated with competition. This motivation, although very effective, is extrinsic. But without competition as part of their musical experience, these students struggle to see a meaningful and worthwhile reason for their effort and commitment. They ask, 'Why am I doing this?' I believe students deserve the opportunity to develop intrinsic motivation…rather than being dependant on others to motivate them, they become self-motivated.*

Knowing that the college bands I was visiting were also fueled by entertainment and not competition, I was curious to discover how other band directors and drumline instructors motivate their students. My question was simply, "How do you get the band/drumline motivated to perform at a high level?" I wanted to know what motivated these bands and drumlines to strive for excellence, to what degree students were self-motivated, and if these top band programs experienced any apathy during the season. What I found after conducting my interviews was a diverse list of motivational tools inherent to the college marching band activity. This list, in part, includes tradition, visiting bands, the success of the football team, travel/trips, bowl games, pride, excellence, empowerment, atmosphere/crowd, arrangements/shows, an alternate system, competitive auditions, friendships, and having fun as some of the main reasons students are motivated to participate in college marching band.

## How Good Do You Want to Be?

At LSU, tradition certainly plays a large role in motivating the band. "Part of it is what came before them," says Frank Wickes. "Every student has to realize that they're marching in a spot in which they're going to be compared to the finest person who's ever marched that spot. And if they think about the traditions of the school and the accolades that have been bestowed on the band from its history—places they've been and the support that people give them—I think a student coming into the band wants to be like that. Everyone holds up LSU as the standard."

LSU also has developed a culture of excellence over a long period of time. This culture motivates students in many ways. "That's part of being in Tiger Band," says Linda Moorhouse. "They see how hard we work. They're dying to be a part of all that. If you don't want to be a part of the program, you don't have to. I will always tell them, 'this class is not required.' If there's a student that's not pulling their weight, that's what I tell the new members and the returning members."

Roy King takes a more direct approach to motivating the band members. As a former member of the band himself, his passion is infectious. King asks, "How good do you want to be?" This is an appeal not only to the band's pride, but to the tradition that has been created at LSU. It asks each individual of the 325 member unit to reflect and ask him/herself how they are going to personally contribute to the tradition of excellence at LSU. The question, "How good do you want to be?" was also made famous by former LSU football coach, Nick Saban.

"We're committed to putting them in a position to be successful," says King. "We're going to do our best to give them music and drill that is appropriate for the next performance based on the rehearsal time that we have. But it's up to them to put forth the effort. It is their band."

At the end of our interview, King touched on the influence the football team has on the band's motivation.

> *In years that the football team is not doing well, I think it's more difficult to motivate them. Sometimes your interest and the number of people who walk through the door have something to do with the success of football. Troy and Jacksonville State are examples of schools where band is the big deal, not football. Those kids know that going in. They're there for another reason—because they think the band is a big deal. At LSU, I think our kids are in the band because they think that band is a big deal, but I think how big of a deal it is has something to do with football. Kids want to perform for an audience and want feedback. The bottom line is if we went into a stadium every Saturday and it was empty, that would have an effect on the morale of the band and then it would be up to us to come up with a different way to motivate them. When the team is winning, it just makes our jobs easier to motivate the band. We don't have to recruit as hard. I think that is the case with most big schools that are successful in football.*

In 2007, LSU won the BCS National Championship, beating Ohio State.

## Demanding Excellence

For Alabama's five drumline instructors, being a great drumline and playing clean are all the motivation they need. Pride, hard work, and high standards define the Alabama Drumline and embracing high expectations are part of being a member. According to Neal Flum, "To some extent they're self-motivated. How the team does and the football game atmosphere and environment motivates them. Warming up on the quad, having a large crowd around generates their willingness to perform at higher levels. I think just demanding it of them and constantly asking them to play at the highest level helps build that. Of course every percussion section is different. They all have a group personality. The leadership this year has made a big difference. Our section leader, Kevin Geiss marched in the Santa Clara Vanguard and is very energetic and personable and pulls everybody along."

Band director Ken Ozzello takes a more intellectual approach and tries to make the band members think about why they are there. He likes to say with a wry smile, "You should only play well if you're interested in being very good."

When I asked the drumline section leaders how they get everyone in their section motivated, they jokingly responded, "Cookies!" (It has been my experience as well that food is the best motivator for college students). They went on to say that "Everybody's motivated, because those who aren't will get 'knocked down' and they don't want to get knocked down anymore."

## It's All about Ownership

At Western Carolina, the marching band operates through a large staff of three directors, staff coordinators, graduate assistants, and section leaders. The band office itself is a large room with four work stations, where open discussions and staff meetings take place. The band directors do not have private offices, but instead prefer a cubicle-style lay-out, creating open space and a welcoming, collaborative environment.

When asked about motivating the band, Bob Buckner almost dismissed it, saying he couldn't remember the last time the band had a poor performance. The reason, he says, is ownership. "I was up in the press box judging at this one particular event. The kids in the office ran the warm-ups and did everything we needed them to do. When it was time for the band to go on the field, they did their thing. That's when they realized that we're saying, it's your band! It's ownership."

The WCU Drumline section leaders pointed to attitude as a motivation tool. "We have to lead by example. If the guys see us hyped up, they get hyped up. It's not that hard getting them hyped up. Before performances, everybody's motivated on their own and it's all about living up to their own expectations." Bass drum section leader Brian Dumas adds, "I have to get them in the happiest mood possible, let them know their drum is ready to play because I worked on it for so long. This way they can be fully confident with their own notes."

## Competitive Spirit

Michigan State's John Madden points to a variety of motivating factors during the season including big games, hosting a visiting band, the atmosphere and crowd, the band's arrangements and shows, travel/trips, a bowl game, self-motivation, a tradition of excellence, and his alternate system. "This is entertainment as big and as grand as it gets," Madden states with conviction. "If you guys do your best, it's going to be as good as anybody can do. This could be the best of college marching band."

Jon Weber also uses different motivational tools with his drumline. "I'm very direct. I'll tell them that where we are now is not good enough. It's the standard. I'll let them know if what they're doing is not up to what Michigan State's drumline is about. I also engage their competitiveness, especially with the "comp-line," which is our competitive indoor drumline. If it's done right, you can prepare them better for life and how to handle the competition. If you look at it that way, it can be a very positive thing. I think the drumline is very self-motivated, but it depends on the show and if they really like it or not. At those points, you give them a little help but you just say, 'I know this isn't what you want to do, but we have a lot to live up to here, and we have to do it.'

"When people show up, the only reason they're here is because they are affected by a very good Michigan State Drumline. They *want to be that* from the get go. That's why they auditioned. All they need is information but the motivation of being good is there for the most part." The competitiveness and motivation level of students interested in becoming a part of the MSU Drumline can be seen in the large number of players who show up for the help sessions during the spring and summer and for auditions. In 2007, MSU had to cut 40 from drumline auditions.

When asked about motivating his peers, drumline section leader Jordan Novak said humbly, "We're really fortunate to have a long history. I think for a while now, we've said we have to be better the next year, or we have to be better than last year. I wouldn't consider this a building program. It's more of one of those sustained type of things."

## Hire the Motivated

To be a member of the Ohio State Marching Band, members have to be self-motivated. The level of desire to march in The Best Damn Band in the Land is extremely high, and auditions are very competitive, turning away 150 students in 2007. As author Steve Chandler says in his excellent book, *100 Ways to Motivate Others*, "The best way for you to have motivated people on your team is to hire self-motivated people." While motivation levels are high at Ohio State, sustaining that motivation over the course of a long college marching band season can still be a challenge.

According to drumline section leader Amanda White, "A lot of it comes later in the week. We know the game is coming up and everyone wants to do well. We know it's going to be exciting. Towards the end of the week, it's not that hard. In the early part of the week, it's harder. Some procrastinate and the focus on drill is lacking. As a leader, I remind people that it's a privilege to be here, and it's their job to march to the best of their abilities on Monday just as they do on Friday.

I try and help people remember that they were picked to be here and made this band because they showed very high potential and have the ability to uphold that standard the entire season. If they're not going to perform to the best of their abilities, I could easily just pull them out. They know, 'If I don't do well, I could get pulled' because we have alternates that learn the show as well. We want to perform well on Saturday, we want to have a good ramp entrance, and there will be tons of people there and we want to do well at skull session because our parents come to that, not to mention visiting bands. It's just about staying consistent."

## Adjusting from Competition

Athletic coach Casey Coleman put it in perspective when he said, "Your toughest competition in life is anyone who is willing to work harder than you." But in the state of Texas, high school marching band is just as competitive as football. According to Nick Williams, "In Texas, on all levels—the arts, athletics—everything is competition-based. In college band, we don't have that. Our competition is ourselves and our reputation. Every year we have between three and five students who just can't do that—they just don't understand this college marching band thing at all. It's usually the non-music majors. They've grown up in a system since sixth grade with beginner band contests. Their whole 7–8 year public school band career is competition-based. I see the benefits of both sides, but it's a challenge."

"In a lot of ways, the band members really are self-motivated. That's the one thing about this place. When they really don't want to work, they know that it's going to be good by the end because all they have to do is turn it on. I think for a lot of the students, the 'having fun' aspect takes the place of the competitive nature of it. Most years the selection of the shows reaches someone at least once. While we're not competitive, the music will be more difficult than what they've ever done in high school."

UNT drumline instructor Frank Nedley points to the realization that the A-line only performs every two years. The marching band drumline performs throughout the fall and is something that prepares them to teach their own line. "I think that's the big thing—to help our music education majors with the teaching aspect and also help them try out for other lines. That's what I try to use to motivate them."

## Up or Out

Former Secretary of State Colin Powell lived by a philosophy with his colleagues in the White House called "Up or Out." This philosophy simply means team members either contribute to the organization in a positive way or they are asked to leave. There is no in between. There are only two options. Up or Out.

As with all great organizations, the Pride of Arizona is filled with people who contribute, make a difference, and are motivated to move the group "up." Arizona band director Jay Rees says, "The kids who stay in the band for 3, 4, 5 years certainly become very self-motivated. They love the experience that they are having, and they want to come back and have that experience again. And over time they recognize that it's now their job to create that environment so the younger members have that experience. I think the freshmen are initially motivated out of fear and being overwhelmed and just going with what the scene is. There are still kids every year who will not come back and decide, 'well that's not for me,' but it's very rare." ▥

# CHAPTER **6**

# Developing Practice Habits

---

"Excellence is not a singular act. You are what
you repeatedly do."—ARISTOTLE

---

Great drumlines and great marching bands are not built on talent alone. In addition to talent, there are many trademarks of greatness that are required to achieve excellence; none more important than practice. According to John Maxwell in his book, *Talent is Never Enough*, "As long as there are people in the world, there will be plenty of talent. If that were enough, everyone would reach their potential. What's missing are things people need in addition to their talent." Maxwell cites thirteen key choices we can make to become a "talent-plus person." Among them are initiative, focus, passion, teachability, perseverance, and practice.

I had several questions in mind when interviewing the band directors and drumline instructors about their students' work ethic and practice habits. What kind of work ethic do other instructors expect? Besides having good players, what other factors influence a high performance level? How do other instructors develop practice habits in their band members? How much individual practice takes place outside of rehearsal?

I was most interested in the factors that were under the students' control—namely work ethic and practice habits. Like choosing to have a positive attitude, how hard you work during rehearsal is always an individual's choice. Regardless of a band's rehearsal schedule or how many shows they perform, a drumline defines their own practice habits and work ethic. As philosopher Robert Pirsig said, "It's so hard when contemplated in advance, and so easy when you do it."

## Veteran Leadership

"There is an immense pride and a strong work ethic in the line," says LSU's Linda Moorhouse. "The drumline has the toughest job because what they do is more intricate in what they have to make happen. They put in extra effort during the season. It's very tough with one-week shows. The students are here to go to school first. The key is trying to make that equation work without sacrificing the student. You can call sectionals all you want, but in the grand scheme of things, they probably won't be fruitful rehearsals."

There is a quote on the wall inside LSU's football stadium that reads, "Outside of yourself, into the team." As I read this quote about what it means to be a team player, it struck me that the LSU Drumline also adopts this team-first attitude when developing practice habits. In addition to work ethic and commitment, the key ingredient to developing good practice habits in an ensemble is accountability. How has assistant section leader Tommy Bowen addressed the importance of everyone being accountable to one another? "Look, we're a drumline," he said. "Why did you audition for this drumline if you're not going to bring yours to the table? We're a family here, and you're letting us down, and we're not all functioning correctly. It's a standard."

LSU section leader Jeremy Logan sees it this way: "In general the work ethic is coming from the old guys. They may say, 'Look, we need to change things and it's up to you to set the standard.' They've done a really good job of that. All the old guys, most of the time, are pretty good at setting a standard and showing the guys this is what we need to do. It's the old adage, 'somebody's always watching, so it's got to be good."

Without question, the challenge the LSU Drumline faces throughout the season is learning, memorizing, and preparing several one-week shows. At the end of the day, a strong work ethic and good practice habits are not only desirable, but required if they are going to put themselves in a position to succeed and play at a high level. According to Logan, "Every show's gradually harder and that's very healthy. When you finally nail it, even though it may be simple, you can feel good that we accomplished this show, we achieved it, now let's move on."

## Balancing Act

As I mentioned in Chapter 2, *Evaluating Expectations*, the Alabama Drumline has an outstanding work ethic. Some of the words I would use to describe their rehearsals are purposeful, focused, intense, demanding, and efficient. It's a cliché, but in a drumline, you really do get out of it what you put into it. The kids at Alabama work very hard, rehearse more than most college bands, and achieve excellence because of it, though their staff is always pushing them to go further.

"Right now it's much better than it has been," says Neal Flum. "On a scale from 1–10, it's a 7. I don't think it's as consistent as it should be, and I don't think the level which it needs to be consistent is there yet either. From time to time there are demonstrations that they understand what we want them to do and they do it, but it's not consistent enough. They get distracted by college—but that's what they're here for!"

Flum continues, "Our practice habits as a group are very good. They continue to evolve as we continue to try and do a better job of teaching them. I don't think they do a good enough job in visual and musical ensemble rehearsal, because I think they get in the mix of the craziness of the band, and they let that affect them and divert them from what it is they really need to be doing. Individually, I'd say 7/10. We could do a lot better job there."

Band director Ken Ozzello is very aware and proud of the fact they he has a first-rate drumline and staff. But with a band of 400 and a drumline of 50, it can be challenging to balance at times. "As far as the drumline's work ethic, it's great," says Ozzello. "It's their own little community. In a small group, you're able to raise expectations. It's small enough that you can manage it. Sometimes they get frustrated that everybody else is not at the same level. But it's like comparing apples and oranges—300 versus 50. I would dare say even in a drum corps, the level of everything is higher in the drumline because you're dealing with a smaller group of people."

When asking the Alabama section leaders about their drumline's practice habits, the students made it clear that their goal was "to get into the ballpark of playing clean all the time" and emphasized personal accountability when memorizing their music. They are also aware that their rehearsal schedule is a lot more demanding than most other schools. "It's frustrating," said one student. "I think this drumline would succeed more with a rehearsal schedule more like other schools. The schedule's rough. But we make it work and balance our lives. You just have to know you're going to have a heavier class load in the spring."

Alabama percussion instructor Michael Keeton understands the balance between practicing and academics can be difficult. He shared his thoughts on the drumline's practice habits and the challenge of balancing musical difficulty with performance quality.

*There are always parameters. You always have to start with the end result in mind. I always try and throw them a bone somewhere, so they can have a little fun with it. You always have to keep what's going fit the music, what's going to work in the time given, and what's going to be the best application to what we're doing, and still try to please everybody with the parts. That's probably one of my biggest concerns, is making sure they're happy with what I give them when I write a chart. As far as practicing, I'd like to see more of it happen. Individuals should get with some of the older guys and practice. They let things go. We need more veteran leadership. However, we rehearse 15 hours a week, so it's tough to practice a lot more than that. They are here to get a degree.*

## Turning up the Heat

In addition to loads of talent, the Western Carolina Drumline exhibits dedication, enthusiasm, and pride in everything they do. While their one-show philosophy helps them play and march at a high level, they work extremely hard and set a very high bar that they try to reach every time they put on their drums.

When asked to describe his drumline's work ethic and practice habits, Matt Henley responded, "I think they are very focused. I think they are very energetic about what they do and they are excited about what they are doing. So the discipline and focus takes care of itself. When everyone wants to be there, those are not issues I deal with."

"As far as practicing outside of rehearsal, I tell them, 'You individually need to get your own reps [repetitions] in. Learning the music and getting their reps in is their responsibility. Some will require more reps than others. They need to find what their rep level is."

I was also curious if the WCU students experienced any apathy throughout the season, and if so, how Matt addressed it. His answer was honest and inspiring:

*About this time in October, focus drifts more towards school (where it should be) and I try and take that into consideration and if I feel like it's time to take it a bit easier on them and not be quite so demanding so they can get through this period of time, I'll do that. But I've actually had a lot more success turning the heat up, having the nerve to stand in front of them and start being more demanding...those attacks, that measure, that tempo, that phrase, even though it would have been pretty good two weeks ago. What I have found, by doing that, with this level of player, is that it sparks new interest, because they just want to be good and they love drumming, and when I start turning it up on them and demanding more, it becomes more interesting to them.*

Bob Buckner also praises the drumline's strong work ethic and gives all the credit to his percussion instructor for building a powerhouse program. "I think it's excellent. First of all these kids really hold Matt in high esteem. They know he knows what he's talking about. They love his writing. I love his writing. For our contest, we have had Bret Kuhn, Dennis DeLucia, and Jim Cassella come in...all the big names. As they come in, one of the things they do is they validate him. Casella just raved to the line about Matt's writing. They have that respect for him. They have developed a pride and a tradition to build on. It's hard to get in our line."

In the past, the WCU Drumline has had a unique system in place to encourage individual practicing. According to the section leaders, "It was common, up until this year, for almost all the drummers to live in the same dorm, so if we had to practice, we would all practice together. In 2006, twenty-seven drummers lived in the same dorm. This year, a lot of us live off campus. Needless to say there's a lot of drumming together. That's our practice—live with somebody!"

## Not the Spartans

There was something about the way Michigan State rehearsed. I couldn't put my finger on it until the Saturday morning rehearsal on game day. After practice was over, I went up to one of the cymbal players and commented, "I'm really impressed with how consistent your work ethic is. Every time you rehearsed something, it was done at a high level. *Every time!* I was waiting for you guys to relax." After giving me his full attention and catching his breath, he simply responded, "Not the Spartans." After that brief but powerful exchange, I realized this work ethic is not only embraced, but *imbedded* in the culture of the Michigan State band members. To put it simply, this is how they do things, and this is the only way they know how to rehearse. When I asked several other band members about this—including one of the students carrying the banner in the parade—they all humbly responded, "Thank you. That's what we try to do."

It sounds so simple.

What are their secrets? Michigan State has developed a culture where this type of work ethic is expected, embraced, and imbedded. When I asked the leaders specifically about the drumline's work ethic and practice habits, it simply reaffirmed what I observed on that Saturday morning.

"I think the drumline's work ethic and dedication is quite obvious," said John Madden. "They're at the top of the chart. I use them as a model for the rest of the band. They're the only section that has a one-hour sectional three days a week. Being in the drumline requires a slightly different investment than memorizing the trumpet part. What the tradition has created is that we also get guys that not only can play, but can *read*. Otherwise they will not survive. There are a lot of college band drummers who have good hands, but they don't read."

When interviewing Jon Weber about the MSU Drumline's work ethic, I found him to be quite sincere and understated. "The work ethic is extremely good. It's obvious they love what they do. That helps a ton. I would describe their work ethic among the best on the campus. It is favorable to any other group that's around on campus. They have a ton of initiative on their own. There are so many of them that do outside drumline activities."

In 2007, Michigan State cut 40 students from drumline auditions. Those who made it buy into the culture and are comprised of a select group of dedicated, committed, and invested percussionists who are also very talented. According to section leader Jordan Novak, "I think our work ethic is decent at times. It progressively gets better the more we work on something they care about. The stuff that I care about is a little different than the stuff that the whole line cares about. You can really tell when things kick in when the whole ensemble is doing what we're supposed to be doing. As for individual practicing, a lot of the practice time that goes on is before and after rehearsal. They have made it a habit to come in at least a half hour a day on their own. That's the average."

Along with work ethic and practice habits, I wanted to know if there were any consequences for *not* practicing and not being prepared. How were students being held accountable? According to Jordan:

> *One of our jobs is to identify that before it happens. Everybody here wants to be here and they're pretty much all committed to the big picture. Usually all it will take is one of us reminding them that they're not fitting in with the ensemble. We'll set a memorization schedule and we set those days enough in advanced so you are going to screw up for a couple days but once Saturday rolls around most of the mistakes have already been made. On Saturday, it should go the other direction. Thursday and Friday is as intense as it gets, so on Saturday we're usually a lot more high-spirited, comments are more positive, and there's a good vibe going—more friendly—and that can keep the spirits going for that really long day. If they don't have it on Saturday, usually getting in somebody's face isn't going to help. If someone's not prepared, you just have to live with it. It used to happen where someone was pulled out for the performance.*

## From Ramp Entrance to Ramp Up

One of the unique aspects of Ohio State's one-week show preparation is what each day looks like in rehearsal. The band members always know what day it is and what needs to be done as they prepare for their performance on Saturday. The practice habits and work ethic at Ohio State are driven by two great traditions—challenges and music checks. Challenges occur every Monday and allow alternates to challenge for a spot in the historic Pregame show. Challenges take place on the practice field and test marching and playing ability. I had the chance to observe the challenges and was thoroughly impressed with the level of discipline, desire, and passion these students put forth as they challenged for a spot. They all gave their best effort and left everything they had on the field.

Music checks occur every Friday and test every aspect of music memorization. The squad leaders play for the staff and the section members play for the squad leaders. If a band member does not pass their music check, there is an appeal process, but if they fail a second time, they do not perform the following week. Needless to say, on Thursday nights in the Steinbrenner Band Center on the campus of The Ohio State University, the work ethic and practice habits of this proud organization are on full display.

When asked about the drumline's work ethic and discipline, instructor Gary Hodges simply said, "It's expected here. We don't have to talk too much about work ethic and discipline." Assistant section leader Scott Pethuyne added, "It's generally good, but the way that our rehearsals are structured, we have a 'ramp up' situation, which sometimes creates a lackadaisical attitude early in the week. Those are some of the most crucial times to be focused and learning, especially with one-week shows. Overall, I think we're pretty much all on the same page and we all want to work hard and we all want to be good. It's just gauging the amount of hard work that will be necessary to be as good as we want to be." Tenor section leader Justin Argentine adds, "We pride ourselves in discipline, tradition, and execution. I think you would be amazed at what it takes to get into the band and what everybody out there has to show to walk in these doors."

## A Legacy of Excellence

For years, the University of North Texas has been considered one of the best college drumlines in the country, primarily due to their success at PASIC (Percussive Arts Society International Convention), outstanding percussion faculty, and national reputation. I was curious to find out to what degree the success of the PASIC drumline translated to the marching band drumline. Did they share the same standards? Did they have the same work ethic and practice habits? Did they play at the same level?

On my first night on campus, I attended rehearsals for both the indoor and outdoor drumlines back to back. What I found is that the two drumlines share some of the same players as well as some similarities and differences. Both drumlines have enormous talent as well as quality instruction. The indoor drumline, or the A-line, directed by Paul Rennick, is known for its legacy of excellence, impeccable execution, and visually entertaining shows. The marching band drumline, or the B-line, directed by graduate and undergraduate students Matt Filosa and Frank Nedley, plays at an extremely high level in their own right, upholding the tradition of excellence that defines North Texas Percussion.

According to marching band director Nick Williams, "With our set up of having graduate and undergraduate students as the drumline's main teachers, they're not as disciplined as the winds looking at it from the outside. As far as the music that they play and their commitment, it's the same or higher. Their sectionals seem a little looser, but it seems to work for the most part. They're on their own more, and I'm with them less."

When asked about the individual practice habits of the drumline members, the UNT instructors stated, "Some do, some don't. Some people can see patterns in music and are familiar with the way we write, so some of the more experienced people can recognize that and not practice a lot. We have some who have a better head on their shoulders, and some who need to practice more than they do."

"What do we do when someone's not prepared? We give a speech. Now, when the internal leaders give a speech, the line really responds to that. We try to tailor the music to the rehearsal time we have and how busy they are, since they're doing so many other things, such as playing in other ensembles."

## Sacrifice

Ready and eager to begin the final week of my journey, I discovered my first day in Tucson was Veteran's Day, canceling classes at the University of Arizona. I decided to take advantage of my day off and play golf with my dad and former professor, Gary Cook, planning to resume my research the following day. When I arrived at the first rehearsal, I was told that the UA Drumline had called a two-hour sectional on Veteran's Day to help prepare for their upcoming performance. That was all I needed to know about the Arizona's Drumline's work ethic and practice habits. I thought to myself, how many other college drumlines would call a sectional on a day that classes were canceled?

In Chapter 2, *Establishing Expectations,* I talked about the University of Arizona's culture of discipline and the high level of focus, energy, and effort Jay Rees expects from his band members. Jay simply said of the drumline's work ethic and practice habits, "It's fantastic. The drumline today is an incredibly efficient, focused, and intense group."

# CHAPTER 7

# Building Musicianship

---

"40% of the music is written down, 60% is not."—DENNIS FISHER

---

For many years, the balance between technique and musicianship has been a passionate issue in marching percussion at all levels. While DCI, WGI, and PAS have successfully showcased the musical potential of the marching percussion ensemble, many college marching band drumlines emphasize teaching technique over teaching music. This can be attributed in part to the culture of college marching band, characterized by its outdoor performances, football atmosphere, and large stadiums. Understanding this culture, I was still curious to find out what musical concepts *were* being taught, taking into account each band's rehearsal time and the number of shows they prepare.

One of the highlights of my travels was interviewing Paul Rennick, a leader in the field of marching percussion and respected by his peers as one of the brightest minds in the activity. Rennick is the Director of the 14-time PAS National Champion University of North Texas Indoor Drumline. In addition, he has been percussion arranger and caption head for the Concord Blue Devils, Sky Ryders, Velvet Knights, Carolina Crown, and Phantom Regiment Drum and Bugle Corps. Rennick was also a design member, music composer/arranger, instructor, and percussion manager for the Tony and Emmy Award winning production, *Blast!* Although Rennick does not teach the marching band drumline at North Texas, I felt his wisdom would benefit readers of this book. As I sat down with Paul for an interview, I asked him to share his philosophy on the state of marching percussion.

One of the themes I took away from our conversation was that Rennick believes there is too much emphasis on technique. He does not use the 3, 6, 9, 12" height system that has been adopted by so many drumline instructors today. "Technique does not equal music," he exclaims. "The height system is not absolute. It depends on the circumstances of music. It's situational." In his teaching, Rennick emphasizes tone production using the piston stroke, full rebound, and control of rebound at different levels while deemphasizing downstrokes.

His philosophy, simply stated, is to start with a musical concept of what you want to sound like. "Start with the music, not the technique," he says. "When you get to the point where it sounds the same, then it will start looking the same."

One of the great stories Paul shared with me was about a competition he judged where he noticed an extra stick bag attached to the snare drums at the two-o'clock position (too far away to use for sticks). He later became aware that there was a twelve-inch ruler sticking up from the bag with heavily lined markings for 3, 6, 9, and 12 inches. Needless to say this incident made a lasting impression on him. He was shocked that an instructor would take teaching technique to such an extreme. Rennick is very humble and is sincerely amazed at the momentum some of the trends have gained in the marching percussion activity. He summed up his philosophy this way:

> *The people that I would consider percussionists and mu-sicians—the people that I have respect for what they do—we all think the same way. The biggest difference for me, with the advent of WGI, which is overwhelmingly the most popular thing, is that it's becoming more than just a musical thing. It's not just a musical activity anymore. It's a multi-media activity. Music is just one small component of the greater thing, which is hard for me because I'm a musician. I do everything—drill writing, visual program—all to support the music. It's always related to the music. I'm much more comfortable listening to a CD of what we do rather than watching it. That's a big difference I think and the way people learn now a days is huge. Music used to be your headphones and stereo. Now it's all labeled to a visual or DVD.*
>
> *That is what is happening to teaching percussion. Teaching percussion now is all visual instruction. It's all about your stick height, your stick movement, and the visual aspects of movement and very few times do you talk about the sound you produce. I think it's a generational*

*thing. I think it goes hand in hand with the barrage of instructional DVDs. I always hear things through my ears. When people talk about a certain group, people won't say, "Remember when they played this?" They'll say, "Remember when they did this?" That's how it's actually remembered. That has gone hand in hand with the way people teach. I teach through sound, through my ears, through the music. My main goal is to counter any of the negative stereotypes. In the past, drumline wasn't only not music, it wasn't even considered real drumming! I have a real love for teaching. That's one of the best things about marching percussion—your ability to teach and affect so many people.*

*The real litmus test for me is this: Is what I'm saying going to be reinforced or agreed with or confirmed by Ed Soph or someone who is a musician? I'm constantly analyzing what I say so it passes that test. I feel like part of the success of what's been going on [at UNT] is the fact that it does apply across the board and it does utilize some common sense approaches and mainly sticks to the ear and it gets them to be better musicians.*

My former professor at the University of Arizona, Gary Cook, always used to tell us, "People listen with their eyes." What a powerful quote! We live in a visual culture where marching band and marching percussion have steadily become a visual performance art first and a musical performance art second. How do we reverse this trend? Heed the words of Paul Rennick: "I'm a musician. I do everything—drill writing, visual program—all to support the music. It's always related to the music."

Paul was also gracious enough to share his views on other values of his philosophy that have helped make the University of North Texas Indoor Drumline the gold standard of college marching percussion ensembles.

**On his leadership style:** *It stems from two things. When I teach I come across as being demanding, yet really pretty nice. I think the reason for that is the way that I put things. In a nutshell, I always instruct them to do what I want them to do and I don't simply describe what they just did wrong. That's a huge thing. Instead, I try and put it this way: 'What I really want you to do is this. I want you to try to think more about this. Can you do that a little more?' And I rarely if ever describe what they just did wrong. So I've created an image of what they're trying to attain.*

**On desire:** *The other thing is I work on their desire level pretty subconsciously. I get them to care about what they're doing as much as possible. And if they care about it more, they will try harder. And if they try harder, they will probably play better. It's a snowball effect. What you'll find is that a lot of my groups are almost self-maintained. You'll hear corrections from people within the line in the same general positive way. When they care about it that much, they communicate that caring in their performance and it affects you.*

**On the state of marching percussion:** *The way things are going now [in the marching percussion activity]; isn't it amazing, how you can see groups that are* *so polished and so clean and so meticulous and yet you feel nothing musically?*

**On rehearsal techniques:** *One of the most effective rehearsal techniques or teaching techniques is when the guys feel and know that they're getting better. They hear it. Then you know you're being effective.*

**On teaching***: If you start on the path of fundamentally knowing your topic, knowing what your goal is, having an image of what you want them to sound like, and then being able to make the corrections that will make a big difference in a short period of time, and you do that in a positive way—there you go.*

I also asked the drumline instructors from the other schools to share their ideas on building musicianship in the marching percussion ensemble. My question was, "What musical concepts do you emphasize the most?" Among the excellent answers were listening, touch, dynamics, balance, sensitivity, phrasing, tempo, timing, interpretation, quality of sound, rhythmic integrity/accuracy, and reading skills. In addition, I inquired if these instructors do any visualization or mental training with their drumlines as part of their performance preparation. At Alabama, Neal Flum uses a visual analogy with dominoes to represent the space between the notes: "When we talk about rhythmic integrity, I ask them to think about their sixteenth notes as dominoes being straight up that have consistent space between them. Sometimes they lean their dominoes in, and that's why it gets ahead.

We never use the terms rushing and dragging. You're either ahead of the beat or behind the beat." Michigan State's Jon Weber added, "We talk about listening to what they're doing compared to whatever their mental image is in their head and tell them to analyze it. It's geared towards their critical thinking. It's really about being aware of the sound that they're putting out."

Renowned sports psychologist Gary Mack proclaimed, "Once you reach a certain level of competency, the mental skills become as important as the physical skills, if not more so." In my article, *Ten Principles for Leading a Quality Marching Percussion Music Rehearsal,* I discuss the art of visualization.

> *Visualization is the process of seeing yourself perform in your mind's eye. Visualization can be done lying in bed, standing in the shower, or sitting in a quiet place, and can also be reinforced during a rehearsal. Comments such as "see yourself playing in uniform," "imagine the crowd," and "visualize the stadium" will get your students mentally focused on their performance. If time allows in rehearsal, it is beneficial to practice visualization together, sitting on the floor, eyes closed, singing through the parts, and seeing yourself having a great performance. This kind of mental practice is often as good or better than playing on the drums.*

Without question, visualization is one of the most valuable and effective mental skills for attaining peak performance and musicianship. A good sports analogy I like to use to teach visualization is the mental training of Baseball Hall of Fame pitcher, Nolan Ryan. According to Ryan in *Mind Gym*,

> *The night before a game I lie down, close my eyes, relax my body, and prepare myself for the game. I go through the entire lineup of the other team, one batter at a time. I visualize exactly how I am going to pitch to each hitter and I see and feel myself throwing exactly the pitches that I want to throw. Before I even begin to warm up at the ballpark, I've faced all of the opposition's hitters four times and I've gotten my body ready for exactly what it is I want to do.*

This story is a tribute to the power of mental training. Although Nolan Ryan possessed enormous talent, a tremendous work ethic, and superior physical skills that led him to the Baseball Hall of Fame, it was his commitment to mental training that helped make him one of the best pitchers the game has ever seen. ■

# CHAPTER 8

# Evaluating Recruiting and Retention

"The band experience is of value to them. Personal value, musical value, not because we're going to a bowl game."—JOHN MADDEN

ow do you keep the cupboard full? How do you build and *maintain* a powerhouse program? How do you motivate students to want to come back every year? Recruiting and retention are critical to any organization's success, whether a company, sports team, or marching band. Recruiting is about selling talented players on coming to your school and joining your team. Retention is about keeping them in your program for the long term. Because an organization's success is directly dependent on the quality of its people, few things are as important as recruiting and retaining the best. According to Ray Davis, author of *Leading for Growth*, "Nothing is more important to the growth of any organization than finding, training, and retaining superior people... Your job is people—period."

In sports and in business, most people will agree that you can't win without good players no matter how strong the leadership. In a college marching band, the same is true. In the bands I observed, there was a plethora of strong players, strong marchers, and above all, strong leaders. In a marching band, bigger is not necessarily better, but given the culture I mentioned in our last chapter, it certainly helps to have a large group playing outdoors in a football stadium seating 90,000 fans. But make no mistake. Quality is more important than quantity, and how a band plays and marches—how it sounds and looks—are the most important qualities of excellence that matter.

What strategies do band directors and percussion instructors employ to recruit the best players to their schools? And more importantly, what attracts students to a band program in the first place? Is it the university, the scholarships, or the chance to fulfill a lifelong dream? Or maybe it is the leader, the band's traditions, or the success of the football team.

Recruiting and retention have great influence on a band's success. Some schools put a lot of effort into it, others very little. Bands such as LSU, Michigan State, and Ohio State impose a cap on its membership and can be more selective in recruiting attitude, commitment, and work ethic as part of the audition process. Other bands like Alabama reached 400 members in 2007, in part due to the hiring of Head Football Coach Nick Saban, which the band directors called "The Saban

Factor." Whatever strategies are used, the goal of successful recruiting and retention is to have a great band, year after year, without missing a beat.

## Show Me the Money

According to Frank Wickes, a lot of Tiger Band's recruiting is due to LSU being a flagship university and the only doctoral granting institution in the state. "It's long established as a quality music school," said Wickes. "Students aspire to come here. We have to spread our recruiting tentacles pretty far, all the way to Texas, South Carolina, and Florida." On average LSU turns away 5-15 students trying out for the drumline each year and 20-25 wind players.

LSU is in a unique position in terms of offering scholarships to their band members. Each LSU bandsman receives a substantial scholarship in the fall every year. This helps both with recruiting and retention, but according to the directors, scholarships are not the reason students want to be a part of the organization. "We are recruiting an entirely different student than we did twenty years ago," says Linda Moorhouse. "Their focus is different and they are serious about their grades. If we told the band that next year we did not have scholarship money, it wouldn't matter to them." However, the staff also recognizes the value of a scholarship beyond financial rewards. "There's prestige in getting a scholarship," says Wickes. "I think we sometimes underestimate that."

Earning a spot in the LSU band is very competitive, instilling pride in the recruiting process and retention of veteran members. Freshmen who want to be in the band have to first pass a music audition. After passing, they are invited to attend band camp. Freshmen have to demonstrate a minimum level to weed out those coming from weaker band programs. "We have returning members that don't make it back every year," states Wickes. "We take the best 325. We have even cut returning music majors before."

## The Saban Factor

As mentioned earlier, "The Saban Factor" was responsible for increasing the Million Dollar Band to 400 members in 2007. With 92,000 fans attending the football team's *spring game* in April, excitement over Alabama football was at its highest point in many years when Nick Saban was hired as head coach.

Inside the school of music, the band staff spends as much time in the high schools as possible. They also present clinics, conduct honor bands, and even host an honor band event on campus. The band staff tries to be selective, recruiting quality students coming to campus. The band also sends out publications and posters and organizes a marching band clinic with guest clinicians, as well as a high school percussion clinic in the summer with over 150 in attendance.

## All in the Family

One of the most remarkable statistics I uncovered in my research was the fact that the Western Carolina Pride of the

Mountains marching band fields 300 members out of an undergraduate student population of only 7,100. This is a tribute to the leadership of Bob Buckner and his staff and the successful recruiting and retention strategies the band has employed.

"Having spent my whole high school teaching career in North Carolina, one of the things I believe in is personal contact," says Buckner. "I do a lot of work with bands during concert festival and I may be the king of all county bands! That's where you really meet kids. They'll pick up pretty quickly whether or not they connect with you."

Buckner's recruiting philosophy differs a bit from some of his colleagues. "We don't go through the acceptance list like many schools. What we do is *we go find kids that we want* and get them to apply to the university. We look for solid leaders and we go after kids in competing bands. The reason for that is nobody else in North Carolina recruits them. Others think they're burned out and don't want to march in college."

Another important recruiting strategy is WCU's commitment to leadership development. "At our leadership camp, we teach things to high school kids that we teach here at WCU," explains Buckner. "We don't just give them information, we teach them hands-on. We also have a drum major academy, a judges training session, and a session on show design. The key to it all is recruiting the band director—getting that person to feel like they're a member of your family. If our leadership is excellent, we have no problem with retention."

Recruiting for the Pride of the Mountains is not just the staff's responsibility. Band members take ownership and initiative to keep the band's momentum going. "The other ingredient," says Buckner, "is we get our kids to make a lot of phone calls. We will work every open house, schedule home visits, and meet one-on-one with students. The last ingredient is after students graduate, I try to stay in touch with them. We'll talk once a month. We are very active in going to the students, to the directors, to the schools, and to other programs."

Without question, WCU's biggest and most successful recruiting effort is hosting and performing at their Tournament of Champions. The TOC is a band contest hosted on the campus of Western Carolina each October featuring more than 20 high school bands. High school students perform for judges and receive feedback and get to see and hear the Pride of the Mountains perform their halftime show. According to Buckner, "75% of the students we recruit are due to the Tournament of Champions exhibitions."

As I discussed in the "Five Factors Influencing Excellence," one of the ways the TOC recruits students is through the band's one-show philosophy. This philosophy allows WCU to focus on cleaning and perfecting one show so they can perform it at an extremely high level in an effort to recruit the best high school musicians in the region. Their show is a sizzling combination of musical, visual, and electronic media.

One of the staples of the Pride of the Mountains is the addition of a five-piece rock band called *Soul Train,* consisting of guitars, bass, drums, and vocals using extensive amplification and a portable stage resembling a tour bus. I found it interesting that the members of *Soul Train* are marching band members, wear marching band uniforms, and attend marching band rehearsals. The incorporation of this group into the halftime show gives the band a unique and distinctive identity and recruits students with contemporary arrangements, state-of-the-art electronics, and stunning visual presentations.

## Beyond a Bowl

Surprisingly, Michigan State's appearance at the 2007 Champs Sports Bowl in Orlando was their first bowl game in many years. Capped at 300 members, the MSU Marching Band has one of the great traditions of excellence in the country. "Michigan State's retention is among the highest in the Big Ten," says band director John Madden. "There are a lot of big college marching bands where kids join because they know they're going to get a big trip. There are a lot of college marching bands that will never go to a bowl, and there's a lot in between. I take pride in the large number of senior level people we keep because the band experience is of value to them. Personal value, musical value, not because we're going to a bowl game. The goals for retention are you are stimulated in the environment and that the environment treats you with respect. That's why you want to come back."

Michigan State's marching band turned 100 kids away in 2007, including 40 from the drumline. Although MSU sends out posters to help recruit, it's really all about the website. "We try identifying and talking to the kids who are already coming here. We send out blanket emails to the incoming class; between 8000-9000 students who are coming. It helps that our visual instructor also works in admissions!"

MSU also takes their band on the road to play at high school exhibitions. Other recruiting strategies their staff employs include judging, running clinics, and guest conducting.

## Identity

In the landscape of college football, one of the greatest re-cruiting advantages one school can have over another is the quality of its facilities. In the world of college marching band, facilities refer primarily to a band room indoors and a practice field outdoors. It is rare for a band to have facilities of such high caliber, but at Ohio State, the Joan Zieg Steinbrenner Band Center certainly fits the bill.

It is nothing less than impressive to walk up the hollowed stairway inside Gate 10 of Ohio Stadium, taking in the painted mural representing all the instruments of the Ohio State band, and entering the Band Center lobby viewing historic uniforms, pictures, and memorabilia from the past. Down the hallway, recruits will discover a wall filled with photos in tribute to the great Ohio State drum majors and most inspirational bandsmen. A little further down sits the trumpet, horn, and percussion practice room, also known as "The Kennel," named for the many cages and instrument lockers used to store the drums. To the left of the main lobby is the enormous band room, showcasing a giant picture of Script Ohio in the background and a NASA-like command center with state-of-the-art technology at the front. This facility is indeed the envy of many other band directors who visit, wishing only for a larger band room and a practice field with grass. Commenting on the recruiting power of the Band Center, band director Jon Woods simply says, "We have a junior/senior night in the spring where we bring them in the door, let them see the facility, and talk to them about the entire band program."

In 2007, Ohio State turned away approximately 150 stu-dents during marching band auditions. Membership in this historic organization is highly valued among OSU students and many want to be a part of the great tradition of "The Best Damn Band in the Land." Besides the fortune of their facilities, the Ohio State staff works very hard at recruiting. "You just can't expect people to walk through the doors and be in the band," explains Woods. "Through our research, seeing and hearing the band live was the top answer to 'why do you want to be in the band?'"

The staff also works closely with the admissions office. "They supply us a list of names of incoming freshmen who were involved with music in high school. We call everybody and find out who the band people are. We pay Kappa Kappa Psi and Tau Beta Sigma [band fraternities] some money to help with this." During the summer, the band directors send out an electronic newsletter and expect squad leaders to keep in touch and communicate with their sections.

Scholarships are used more for retention than recruiting and are given to 4th and 5th year seniors. "We reward longevity," says Woods. "To be eligible for a scholarship, students need to maintain a 3.0 or better, receive a B or A playing grade, and have a good marching score. The retention rate is very high and has been very important to our success. Usually once a student makes this band, they stay for 5 years. Scholarships have helped at the 5th year level." It also helps to be a senior tuba player, as the tradition of "Dotting the 'i" in *Script Ohio* is one of the most prestigious honors and most effective recruiting practices anywhere in college marching band.

In today's WGI and DCI dominated culture of marching percussion, one might wonder why so many students want to play in a drumline that is so traditional where the drums are still carried by slings and the heads are made of mylar. I asked a few of the drumline members, "Why are you interested in marching with Ohio State?"

Lamar Bland, who plays snare in the Ohio State Drumline, also marched with the Glassmen and Capital Regiment Drum and Bugle Corps as well as an area indoor drumline. When I asked him this question, I found his answer refreshing. He said he is open-minded about different styles of drumming. He enjoys the games, and enjoys both styles of drumming. One *or* the other doesn't fulfill him. He considers himself a well-rounded percussionist. He is also interested in the show band style. Needless to say, his DCI friends can't understand the attraction to the OSU experience. "I don't have time to explain it to them," says Lamar. "It's about culture, tradition, and identity!"

Drew Riedel, who is the bass drum section leader, came to Ohio State all the way from Mesa, Arizona. Drew played in a competitive marching band at Dobson High School with a corps-style/one-show philosophy common in today's high school band culture. Certainly, Ohio State is the opposite of Drew's high school experience. Drew said he likes marching with Ohio State because he is always fighting for his spot and because he respects the efficiency, level, and traditions of the band. Drew explains, "People love this band. We're treated like celebrities. I also have a pride and love for Ohio State, and this is Ohio State's band. The band has rich traditions, like the Ramp entrance, *Script Ohio* and *Hang on Sloopy*, and I love football. Plus, when I saw the band live, I said, 'I want to do that!"

Why does OSU's Drumline still play in the traditional style? According to drumline instructor Gary Hodges:

*The drum height, and therefore the use of slings are driven by the [band's high-step] marching style. All of the band members are expected to perform the same marching maneuvers. The bass drum [mallet] twirls were driven by the pregame silent entrance and the cadence to bring the band on the field so the basses would have a visual reference for staying together, especially with the loud crowd noise. I believe that the mylar heads were just a preference, and a determination NOT to follow current trends [in order] to maintain tradition, and also the importance of not having to carry the extra weight the high tension drums require.*

## Reputation

Recruiting and retention are a little different at the University of North Texas. "We honestly don't do very much recruiting at all just because of the name and reputation of the school," says band director Nick Williams. The applied teachers do the recruiting. Our exhibitions also help, as well as the CDs we do. Our registrars office gives us a list of students who have band experience and we contact those students. If I'm in town, I also speak at every freshmen orientation session about the band."

UNT has a three-year requirement for music majors to march. In 2007, 210 of the 260 marching band members were music majors and 190 of those were music education majors. There were only 50 non-majors in the band. According to Williams, "If there was no requirement for music majors, coupled with the number of opportunities to play in all the other ensembles, we would have a band of 100. Can you imagine North Texas, the largest College of Music in the country, having 100 people in the marching band?"

## Training Day

Several bands such as Western Carolina, Michigan State, Ohio State, and Arizona offer help sessions or drumming classes to help recruit numbers and talent. At WCU, part of the drumline's development is a voluntary drumming session that is held once a week from January to the end of April where students come when they can and high school students are invited to attend.

At Michigan State, drumline help sessions take place once a week during the spring semester. "The goals of the help sessions are to improve the general quality of drumming in the area and try to educate the programs in the state," says Jon Weber. "The help sessions are a chance for high school students to get acclimated to MSU and see if it's something they want to be a part of. It's also a chance for them to meet our section leaders and it gives those leaders a chance to teach. I'll go around to the different sections and watch and give them helpful hints about how to approach certain situations so they get a better idea of how to handle things. How often as a teacher do you get a chance to watch your students teach and give them hints?" According to Weber, "We started the help sessions largely because we had so many students who wanted to be in the line, but many of them came from high schools that didn't have the same kind of instruction, so it didn't seem fair. The disparity was incredible. So we just started it to help out. But then I found other ways to make it useful for different reasons."

At Ohio State, their help sessions involve the entire band and are called "summer sessions," taking place every Tuesday and Thursday evening in June, July, and August. The purpose of the summer sessions is to teach the fundamentals to prospective new members and to get them ready for auditions. According to a squad leader, "It started with approximately 6-7 students that were on campus for summer school and one of us just said, 'Let's start getting ready for marching band.'" In the summer of 2007, an average of 170 people attended each session. Summer sessions are always student run and are all volunteer. Students take great pride in teaching the new people what they need to know to make the band. The student leaders create a syllabus for what they're going to cover at each session and they also get feedback from one of their directors attending each session. The directors attend two weeks at a time on a rotational basis throughout the summer.

The Arizona drumline offers a drumming class in the spring as well as one camp in June and one camp in July leading up to auditions in August. According to the section leaders, "It is getting more and more competitive due to the spring class and summer camps."

## Recruiting and Retention: Excellent Practices from the Leaders

▶ Adjudication
▶ Arrangements/shows
▶ Attending a football game

- ▶ Band DVD
- ▶ Band's reputation
- ▶ Band travel/trips
- ▶ Bowl game
- ▶ Calling students
- ▶ Campus visits
- ▶ CDs, brochures, posters
- ▶ Drum major camp
- ▶ Emails to incoming freshmen
- ▶ e-newsletter
- ▶ Environment based on respect
- ▶ Equipment
- ▶ Facilities
- ▶ Family atmosphere
- ▶ Friendships
- ▶ Guest conducting
- ▶ High school exhibitions
- ▶ High school percussion camp
- ▶ Home visits
- ▶ Host honor band/concert festival w/guest clinician
- ▶ Hosting a Band Day or Tournament of Champions
- ▶ Keeping in touch with students after they graduate
- ▶ Leadership camp
- ▶ Leadership opportunities
- ▶ Personal contact with high school band directors
- ▶ Providing a band experience of value—musically, socially, and personally
- ▶ Scholarships
- ▶ School traditions
- ▶ Senior day

- ▶ Spring/summer help sessions
- ▶ Staff/directors
- ▶ Success of football team
- ▶ Reputation of university/school of music
- ▶ Tradition/culture of excellence
- ▶ Website
- ▶ Working with admissions ◾

# CHAPTER 9

# Crunching the Numbers

"That's what our work is about: building a framework of greatness, articulating timeless principles that explain why some become great and others do not."—JIM COLLINS

Let's review. Culture, staff and student leadership, rehearsal time, number of shows, and competitive auditions. These are the five factors that influence excellence in a college marching band. In addition to these key factors, I have included in this chapter statistical data and research from the 2007 season that contribute in unique ways to the success of these band programs. Items included are: rehearsal schedules, number of halftime shows, band size, percentage of music majors, undergraduate student population, instrumentation, and marching band requirements.

## Louisiana State University

- ▶ Band rehearses T–F 3:50–5:20pm, no drumline warm-up prior
- ▶ Drumline rehearses M 7:00–9:00pm
- ▶ Game day rehearsal lasts 2-hours/drumline meets 2–3 hours prior
- ▶ 5–6 shows
- ▶ 325 band members, 20% music majors, 24,000 undergraduate students
- ▶ Instrumentation: 9 Snares, 6 Tenors, 6 Basses, 9 Cymbals, 0 Pit
- ▶ No marching band requirement for majors

## University of Alabama

- ▶ Band rehearses M–F 4:00–5:30pm
- ▶ Drumline rehearses M–F 3:30–4:20pm & W 6:30–9:30pm
- ▶ Game day rehearsal lasts 2-hours/drumline meets 30 minutes prior
- ▶ 3 shows
- ▶ 400 band members, 15% music majors, 21,000 undergraduate students
- ▶ Instrumentation: 11 Snares, 6 Tenors, 6 Basses, 13 Cymbals, 14 Pit
- ▶ One year marching band requirement for majors

## Western Carolina University

- ▶ Band rehearses MWF 3:45–5:45pm, drumline warms up at 3:45
- ▶ Drumline rehearses M 6:00–7:15pm (first half of season)
- ▶ Game day rehearsal lasts 2 hours/drumline meets 30 minutes prior
- ▶ 1 show
- ▶ 300 band members, 32% music majors, 7,100 undergraduate students
- ▶ Instrumentation: 10 Snares, 5 Tenors, 6 Basses, 12 Cymbals, 15 Pit
- ▶ Two year marching band requirement for majors

## Michigan State University

- ▶ Band rehearses M–F 4:30–6:00pm & M 7:00–9:00pm
- ▶ Drumline rehearses MWF 3:30–4:30pm
- ▶ Game day rehearsal lasts 2 hours/drumline meets 60 minutes prior
- ▶ 6 shows
- ▶ 300 band members, 10% music majors, 36,000 undergraduate students
- ▶ Instrumentation: 10 Snares, 5 Tenors, 7 Basses, 8 Cymbals, 0 Pit
- ▶ No marching band requirement for majors

## Ohio State University

- ▶ Band rehearses M–F 4:00–6:00pm
- ▶ Drumline calls extra sectionals when needed
- ▶ Game day rehearsal lasts 2 hours/drumline meets 90 minutes prior
- ▶ 7 shows
- ▶ 225 band members, 25% music majors, 39,000 undergraduate students
- ▶ Instrumentation: 14 Snares, 4 Tenors, 4 Basses, 5 Cymbals, 0 Pit
- ▶ No marching band requirement for majors

## University of North Texas

- ▶ Band rehearses MWF 4:15–6:15pm, drumline warms up at 3:45
- ▶ Drumline rehearses T 6:15–8:15pm
- ▶ Game day rehearsal lasts 1.5 hours
- ▶ 2–3 shows
- ▶ 260 band members, 80% music majors, 27,000 undergraduate students
- ▶ Instrumentation: 10 Snares, 5 Tenors, 6 Basses, 10 Cymbals, 10 Pit
- ▶ Three year marching band requirement for majors

## University of Arizona

- ▶ Band rehearses MWF 3:00–5:00pm, F 7:00–10:00pm, Sat. 8:00am–12:00pm
- ▶ Drumline meets MWF at 2:40pm and has sectionals during these rehearsal times as determined by their instructors.
- ▶ 1 show
- ▶ 270 band members, 15% music majors, 29,000 undergraduate students
- ▶ Instrumentation: 8 Snares, 4 Tenors, 6 Basses, 9 Cymbals, 4 Pit
- ▶ No marching band requirement for majors

## A Word for the Educator

Actor Martin Sheen, in his role as U.S. President Jed Bartlet on the TV drama, *The West Wing,* would often conclude an episode with the question, "What's next?" Sheen's tone was always uplifting; one of confidence, passion, and purpose, determined to lead the American people to a better future. Now that you have read, *Marching Bands and Drumlines: Secrets of Success from the Best of the Best* and have access to seven of the top college marching bands and drumlines in the country, what's next? What's next for you as an educator? What's next for your program? What's next for your students?

The topics discussed in this book—setting goals, establishing expectations, teaching life lessons, studying leadership styles, instilling motivation, developing practice habits, building musicianship, evaluating recruiting and retention, and crunching the numbers—have always been, and always will be, real issues that determine whether a marching band achieves excellence or falls short of it. Like an iceberg, these topics lie below the surface and establish a rock-solid foundation. They cannot be seen by the casual observer, but without them, the structure becomes weak and eventually starts to fall apart. The top of the iceberg rises above the surface for all to see and includes what most people associate with marching band—music, drill, pep rallies, parades, football games, and even competition.

In my article, *Reading is Not Optional,* I state, "As educators, we have the power to choose what we teach and how we teach it. For the most part, our teaching is directly connected to what we believe in, our values, and our philosophy. Sometimes, it is not what we teach that is the problem, but what we leave out." It is my hope that these seven outstanding bands and the people who lead them have inspired you to choose to tap into the bottom of the iceberg a little more. If you do, I think you will start to uncover something very special. ▧

# Bibliography

Brown, Bruce. *1001 Motivational Messages and Quotes for Athletes and Coaches.* Coaches Choice. 2001.

Buyer, Paul. "Balancing Musical Difficulty with Performance Quality." *Percussive Notes.* 2002.

Buyer, Paul. "Lessons Learned On and Off the Field." *Percussive Notes.* 2003.

Buyer, Paul. "Reading is Not Optional." *Percussive Notes.* 2007.

Buyer, Paul. "Teaching the Values of Competition." *Teaching Music.* 2005.

Buyer, Paul. "Ten Principles for Leading a Quality Marching Percussion Rehearsal." *Percussive Notes.* 2006.

Chandler, Steve. *100 Ways to Motivate Others.* The Career Press, Inc. 2008.

Collins, Jim. *Good to Great and the Social Sectors.* Jim Collins. 2005.

Curtis, Brian. *Every Week a Season.* Ballantine Books. 2004.

Davis, Ray. *Leading for Growth.* Wiley, John & Sons, Inc. 2007.

Dorfman, H.A. *Coaching the Mental Game.* Taylor Trade Publishing. 2003.

Harari, Owen. *The Leadership Secrets of Colin Powell.* McGraw-Hill. 2003.

Hast, Dorothea, James Cowdery, and Stan Scott. *Exploring the World of Music.* Kendall Hunt Publishing Company. 1997.

Janssen Jeff. "How You Can Breakout and Breakthrough to the Next Level." *ChampionshipCoachesNetwork.com.* 2007.

Janssen, Jeff. "Commitmment Continuum." *Championship-CoachesNetwork.com.* 2006-2007.

Krzyzewski, Mike. *Beyond Basketball.* Warner Business Books. 2006.

Mack, Gary. *Mind Gym.* Contemporary Books/McGraw-Hill. 2001.

Maxwell, John. *Talent is Never Enough.* Thomas Nelson, Inc. 2007.

Miller, Robin. Untitled. *2theadvocate.com.* Capital City Press LLC. 2007.

# About the Author

**PAUL BUYER** is Director of Percussion, Director of Music, and Associate Professor of Music at Clemson University. Prior to his appointment at Clemson, Dr. Buyer served as Assistant Director of Bands and Coordinator of Percussion at Garland High School in Garland, Texas. He received his Doctor of Musical Arts and Master of Music degrees from The University of Arizona and his Bachelor of Science degree from Ball State University. Dr. Buyer is a contributing author to the second edition of *Teaching Percussion* by Gary Cook and his articles have appeared in the *American Music Teacher, Teaching Music,* and *Percussive Notes*. He is a former member of the Star of Indiana Drum and Bugle Corps and placed 2nd in DCI Keyboard Individuals in 1990. In 1992, he was a percussion staff member with the Dutch Boy Drum and Bugle Corps. Dr. Buyer serves as a clinician/endorser for Remo Drumheads, Sabian Cymbals, Pro-Mark Drumsticks, and is a consultant for Mike Balter Mallets. He is a member of the Percussive Arts Society's Marching Percussion and College Pedagogy Committees and is chair of the PAS Education Committee.